Let's Pray About It

Pamela Govender

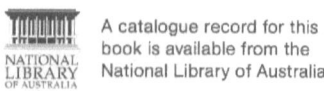
A catalogue record for this book is available from the National Library of Australia

Copyright © 2025 Pamela Govender
All rights reserved.
ISBN-13: 978-1-923174-45-0

Linellen Press
265 Boomerang Road
Oldbury, Western Australia
www.linellenpress.com.au

In Loving Memory

In loving memory of my younger brother, Rodney Naidoo. Your light continues to inspire and guide me. May this book, *Let's Pray About It,* serve as a testament to your enduring spirit and the eternal bond we share. Through these prayers, may others find the solace, strength, and hope that you always encouraged me to seek. You are forever in my heart, and your presence is deeply missed. Love you always.

Other books by this author

I Smiled Today

Contents

In Loving Memory iii

Contents v

Acknowledgements 1

How to Effectively Use This Book 3

How to Pray Effectively with Faith. 5

The Significance of the Anointing Oil 7

Symbol of God's Presence and Power 7

Healing and Restoration 8

Consecration and Dedication 8

Symbol of Joy and Blessing 9

Unity and Communion 9

Faith and Obedience 10

The Importance of Fasting and Praying 10

Seeking God's Guidance and Will 11

Repentance and Spiritual Renewal 11

Spiritual Discipline and Focus 12

Overcoming Spiritual Strongholds 12

Aiding in Deliverance and Breakthrough 13

Humbling Oneself Before God 13

Deepening Intimacy with God 14

The Lord's Prayer 15

Prayer and the Life of Jesus 19
Jesus' Prayer Life.. 22
Old and New Testament Miracles and Testimonies: 24
Understanding the Holy Spirit 28
The Power of Intercession 36
The Prayer of Jabez 38
The Ten Commandments: 41
A Guide for Living 41
Prayer of Salvation 45
Prayer over Anointing Oil 51
Prayer to Wear the Full Armour of God 60
Prayer for Unwavering Faith 67
Prayer for Myself 73
An Everyday Prayer 82
A Prayer for Overcoming Negativity 89
Prayer for My Children 95
Prayer for Healing 102
Prayer for Healing, Strength, and Divine Intervention 110
Prayer for Unemployment 118
Prayer for Our Marriage 126
Prayer for all Men in our Lives 134

Prayer for all Women in our Lives 140

Prayer Over Debt and Finances 145

Prayer Over my Business 152

Prayer for Anxiety and Depression 158

Prayer for Thanks and Gratitude 164

Powerful Prayer to Break Generational Curses 172

Prayer for Peace 180

Prayer for a Peaceful Sleep 186

Praying against Addictions 192

Prayer for Mourning and Grieving 198

Prayer to Unleash Miracles and Blessings over My Life 204

A Powerful Prayer over Anger, Resentment, Bitterness 210

Praying for Children Who Are Missing 215

Prayer for my Children During Exams 222

Prayer for our World 230

Prayer for Women Seeking the Gift of Motherhood 236

A Prayer for Discovering and Using Gifts and Talents 244

A Prayer for Forgiveness 250

A Prayer for Overcoming Fear 256

A Prayer for Compassion 262

A Prayer for Unity and Harmony in Family 268

Prayer for Activating the Fruit of the Spirit 274

Prayer for my Strength and Support as a FIFO Worker 282

The Importance of Praise, Worship, and Prayer 289

Why We Should Praise and Worship 290

A Special Message to You 292

Powerful way to Overcome Life's Struggles 295

About the Author 325

Acknowledgements

To my beloved husband, Seelan, your unwavering support and love have been the foundation upon which this book was built. Your encouragement and belief in me have been my strength throughout this journey.

To my dear sons, Kaylan and Nikel, you are my constant source of inspiration and joy. Your patience, understanding, and love have not only made this journey possible but have also enriched every step of it. I am deeply grateful for the way you continually support and uplift me. Your presence in my life is a cherished blessing that I thank God for every day.

To my late parents who taught us to find a friend in Jesus at a young age, believing in the wisdom of Proverbs 22:6: "Train up a child in the way he should go; even when he is old, he will not depart from it." Your faithfulness and guidance continue to shape my life and work.

To all the members of our Facebook page, *Let's Pray About It*, your faith, dedication, and support have been a source of immense encouragement. Thank you for being a part of this community and for sharing in this journey of faith and prayer.

With deepest gratitude,

Pamela Govender

How to Effectively Use This Book

Daily Prayer and Reflection: Start each day by choosing a prayer that aligns with your current struggles or situations, letting the words deeply resonate within you. Reflect on the accompanying *Word of Encouragement* and scripture *Verse*, drawing strength and hope from them as you consider their relevance to your life.

Journaling: Document your thoughts and any messages you receive in your journal, noting your feelings, breakthroughs, and how you observe God working in your life. Document your journey and growth in faith.

Anointing Oil: Use the oil as you pray, especially when seeking healing, blessing, or protection. Let it remind you of God's power and presence.

Fasting and Praying: Dedicate specific times to fast and pray for deeper connection and spiritual breakthroughs. Combine this with reading the Bible and listening to praise and worship music.

Scripture Study: Read the Bible verses provided for each prayer to deepen your understanding and build your faith. Let God's Word guide your prayers.

Praise and Worship: Integrate praise and worship into your prayer routine to invite God's presence and uplift your spirit.

By consistently integrating these elements into your routine, you will cultivate a deeper connection with God, gain strength and hope through His Word, and experience spiritual breakthroughs. Let this book be your companion as you navigate life's challenges, drawing on its guidance and encouragement to grow in faith and walk closely with God each day.

How to Pray Effectively with Faith.

Prayer is a relationship-building activity that deepens your connection with God. By praying with faith, aligning with His will, and trusting in His promises, you can experience the peace and power that come from knowing you are communicating with your loving Heavenly Father.

Praying effectively with faith, based on scripture, involves aligning our prayers with God's will and promises:

Believe in God's Presence: Hebrews 11:6 reminds us that faith requires believing that God exists and rewards those who seek Him earnestly.

Sincerity and Honesty: Psalm 145:18 encourages us that the Lord is near to all who call on Him in truth, emphasising the importance of sincerity in prayer.

Trust in God's Will: Proverbs 3:5-6 teaches us to trust in the Lord with all our heart and lean not on our own understanding, acknowledging His wisdom and sovereignty.

Use Scripture: Ephesians 6:17-18 advises us to pray in the Spirit on all occasions with all kinds of prayers and requests, and to keep alert with perseverance.

Persistency: Luke 18:1 teaches us about the parable of the persistent widow, showing the importance of persevering in prayer and not giving up.

Gratitude: Philippians 4:6 instructs us to present our requests to God with thanksgiving, recognising His goodness and provision.

Confession and Forgiveness: 1 John 1:9 assures us that if we confess our sins, God is faithful and just to forgive us and cleanse us from all unrighteousness.

Listen: James 1:5-6 encourages us to ask God for wisdom and to believe without doubting, knowing that He gives generously to all without finding fault.

By following these biblical principles, we can pray with faith, trusting that God hears our prayers, aligning our hearts with His will, and growing deeper in our relationship with Him.

The Significance of the Anointing Oil

Anointing oil in the Christian faith is not merely a symbolic act but a practice rooted in scripture that signifies God's presence, healing, consecration, blessing, and the believer's faith and obedience to His divine will. Its significance underscores the spiritual truths and principles found throughout the Bible concerning God's sovereignty and His desire to bless and sanctify His people.

Symbol of God's Presence and Power

In the Old Testament, anointing with oil was a visible sign of God's chosen ones. For instance, Samuel anointed David with oil to signify his selection as king:

"So, Samuel took the horn of oil and anointed him in the presence of his brothers, and from that day on the Spirit of the Lord came powerfully upon David." — **1 Samuel 16:13 (NIV)**

This act symbolised the empowerment and presence of the Holy Spirit in David's life.

Healing and Restoration

The New Testament instructs believers to use anointing oil as part of the healing process. James writes:
"Is anyone among you sick? Let them call the elders of the church to pray over them and anoint them with oil in the name of the Lord. And the prayer offered in faith will make the sick person well; the Lord will raise them up. If they have sinned, they will be forgiven." — **James 5:14-15 (NIV)**
This practice signifies faith in God's ability to bring physical and spiritual healing, acknowledging His sovereign authority over sickness and disease.

Consecration and Dedication

In the Old Testament, anointing oil was used to consecrate priests and the tabernacle, setting them apart for God's service:
"Then the Lord said to Moses, 'Take the following fine spices: 500 shekels of liquid myrrh, half as much (that is, 250 shekels) of fragrant cinnamon, 250 shekels of fragrant calamus, 500 shekels of cassia—all according to the sanctuary shekel—and a hint of olive oil. Make these into a sacred anointing oil, a fragrant blend, the work of a perfumer. It will be the sacred anointing oil. Then use it to anoint the tent of meeting, the ark of the covenant law, the table and all its articles, the lampstand and its accessories, the altar of incense, the altar of burnt offering and all its utensils, and the basin with its stand. You shall consecrate them so they will be most holy, and whatever touches them will be holy.'" — **Exodus 30:22-29 (NIV)**
This oil was reserved for sanctifying God's chosen servants and places.

Symbol of Joy and Blessing

Anointing with oil is also a gesture of honour and blessing. The psalmist writes:
"You prepare a table before me in the presence of my enemies. You anoint my head with oil; my cup overflows." — **Psalm 23:5 (NIV)**
This symbolises divine favour, provision, and joy overflowing in the presence of God.

Unity and Communion

Anointing oil is used in communal and sacramental contexts within the Christian church, marking significant moments in a believer's journey of faith and dedication to God, such as during baptism, confirmation, and other rituals. The psalmist speaks to the beauty of unity among God's people:
"How good and pleasant it is when God's people live together in unity! It is like precious oil poured on the head, running down on the beard, running down on Aaron's beard, down on the collar of his robe." — **Psalm 133:1-2 (NIV)**

Faith and Obedience

Anointing with oil is a demonstration of faith in God's promises and obedience to His Word. It reflects trust in His power to fulfil His purposes and bring about His will in the lives of believers. As the psalmist declares:

"But my horn you have exalted like a wild ox; I have been anointed with fresh oil." — **Psalm 92:10 (NIV)**

By understanding and embracing the significance of anointing oil, you can deepen your spiritual walk and experience the fullness of God's blessings, healing, and sanctification in their lives.

The Importance of Fasting and Praying

Fasting and praying are integral spiritual disciplines in Christianity that facilitate seeking God's will, repentance, spiritual renewal, overcoming spiritual strongholds, aiding in deliverance, humbling oneself before God, and deepening intimacy with Him. These practices are rooted in scripture and are essential for spiritual growth, discernment, and experiencing God's power and presence in our lives.

Seeking God's Guidance and Will

Fasting and praying are often linked with seeking God's guidance and discernment. In Acts, we see the leaders in Antioch fasting and praying before commissioning Paul and Barnabas for their missionary journey, demonstrating a reliance on God's direction:

"While they were worshiping the Lord and fasting, the Holy Spirit said, 'Set apart for me Barnabas and Saul for the work to which I have called them.' So after they had fasted and prayed, they placed their hands on them and sent them off." — **Acts 13:2-3 (NIV)**

Repentance and Spiritual Renewal

Fasting is associated with repentance and turning away from sin. The prophet Joel calls for fasting as a sign of returning to God with all one's heart, accompanied by weeping and mourning, emphasising a posture of humility and contrition:

"'Even now,' declares the Lord, 'return to me with all your heart, with fasting and weeping and mourning.'" — **Joel 2:12 (NIV)**

Spiritual Discipline and Focus

Jesus fasted for forty days in the wilderness before beginning His ministry, demonstrating the importance of spiritual discipline and focus:

"Then Jesus was led by the Spirit into the wilderness to be tempted by the devil. After fasting forty days and forty nights, he was hungry." — **Matthew 4:1-2 (NIV)**

Fasting enhances spiritual discipline, allowing believers to focus more intently on prayer, spiritual matters, and drawing closer to God.

Overcoming Spiritual Strongholds

Some spiritual challenges or obstacles are overcome through fasting and prayer. Jesus taught about the disciples' inability to cast out certain demons except through prayer and fasting:

"However, this kind does not go out except by prayer and fasting." — **Matthew 17:21 (NKJV)**

"So He said to them, 'This kind can come out by nothing but prayer and fasting.'" — **Mark 9:29 (NKJV)**

Aiding in Deliverance and Breakthrough

The book of Esther highlights fasting as a communal act that led to deliverance and victory over enemies. Esther calls for a fast to seek God's intervention in a time of crisis:

"Go, gather together all the Jews who are in Susa, and fast for me. Do not eat or drink for three days, night or day. I and my attendants will fast as you do. When this is done, I will go to the king, even though it is against the law. And if I perish, I perish." — **Esther 4:16 (NIV)**

Humbling Oneself Before God

Fasting involves denying oneself physical comforts to humble oneself before God. The psalmist describes fasting as an act of mourning and humility, recognising our dependence on God's mercy and grace:

"Yet when they were ill, I put on sackcloth and humbled myself with fasting. When my prayers returned to me unanswered." — **Psalm 35:13 (NIV)**

Deepening Intimacy with God

Fasting and praying deepen one's intimacy with God by fostering a deeper connection through spiritual discipline and reliance on His strength and provision. Isaiah speaks of fasting that pleases God and results in blessings:

"Is not this the kind of fasting I have chosen: to loose the chains of injustice and untie the cords of the yoke, to set the oppressed free and break every yoke? Is it not to share your food with the hungry and to provide the poor wanderer with shelter—when you see the naked, to clothe them, and not to turn away from your own flesh and blood? Then your light will break forth like the dawn, and your healing will quickly appear; then your righteousness will go before you, and the glory of the Lord will be your rear guard." —
Isaiah 58:6-8 (NIV)

By understanding and practicing fasting and praying, you can deepen your spiritual walk, experience God's guidance, and witness His power in their lives.

The Lord's Prayer

(Matthew 6:9-13)

Our Father who art in heaven,
hallowed be thy name.
Thy kingdom come.
Thy will be done
on earth as it is in heaven.
Give us this day our daily bread,
and forgive us our trespasses,
as we forgive those who trespass against us,
and lead us not into temptation,
but deliver us from evil.
For thine is the kingdom
and the power, and the glory,
forever and ever.
Amen.

The Lord's Prayer is a foundational Christian prayer that provides a model for how to pray. Let's unpack it to understand its deeper meaning and significance.

"Our Father who art in heaven,"

- **God as Our Father:** We begin by addressing God as our loving Father, highlighting a personal and intimate relationship. Acknowledging that God is in heaven, we recognise His transcendence and sovereign authority over all creation.

"Hallowed be thy name."

- **Honouring God's Name:** We declare God's name as holy, showing reverence and respect. This line emphasises our desire to honour and glorify God in all we do.

"Thy kingdom come."

- **Desiring God's Rule:** We express a longing for God's kingdom to be established on earth. This reflects our hope for a world governed by God's justice, peace, and love.

"Thy will be done on earth as it is in heaven."

- **Seeking God's Will:** We pray for God's will to be accomplished on earth just as it is perfectly fulfilled in heaven. This line teaches us to align our desires and actions with God's purposes.

"Give us this day our daily bread,"

- **Dependence on God:** We ask God to provide for our daily needs, acknowledging our reliance on Him for sustenance and provision. This line encourages trust in God's continuous care.

"And forgive us our trespasses, as we forgive those who trespass against us,"

- **Seeking Forgiveness:** We request God's forgiveness for our sins, recognising our need for His mercy.

- **Forgiving Others:** We commit to forgiving those who have wronged us, reflecting the reciprocal nature of forgiveness. This teaches us the importance of grace and compassion.

"And lead us not into temptation, but deliver us from evil."

- **Asking for Guidance:** We seek God's help in avoiding temptation and making righteous choices.

- **Protection from Evil:** We request God's protection from all forms of evil and harm, acknowledging our need for His safeguarding power.

"For thine is the kingdom, and the power, and the glory, forever and ever. Amen."

- **Praising God:** We conclude by affirming God's eternal sovereignty, power, and glory. This expression of praise reaffirms our faith in God's ultimate authority and majesty, ending the prayer with a strong statement of praise.

Summary

The Lord's Prayer serves as a comprehensive guide for our prayer life, teaching us to honour God, seek His will, rely on His provision, ask for forgiveness, extend forgiveness to others, seek guidance, and trust in His protection. It concludes with an expression of praise that acknowledges God's eternal reign and glory. By praying this prayer, we align our hearts with God's purposes and draw closer to Him in our daily lives.

Prayer and the Life of Jesus

Prayer was a central aspect of Jesus' life and teachings, providing a profound example for His followers. By examining Jesus' teachings on prayer and specific instances of His own prayer life, we can gain a deeper understanding of the importance and power of prayer.

Jesus' Teachings on Prayer

1. **The Lord's Prayer (Matthew 6:9-13, Luke 11:2-4)**
   Jesus provided a model prayer, commonly known as the Lord's Prayer, which encompasses praise, petition, and confession.

   - **Content:** The prayer begins with reverence for God ("Our Father in heaven, hallowed be your name"), aligns with His will ("Your kingdom come, your will be done"), asks for daily needs ("Give us today our daily bread"), seeks forgiveness ("Forgive us our debts"), and requests protection from evil ("Lead us not into temptation, but deliver us from the evil one").

   - **Significance:** This prayer serves as a comprehensive guide for approaching God, emphasising the importance of aligning our desires with God's will and seeking His guidance and provision.

2. **Persistence in Prayer (Luke 18:1-8)** In the Parable of the Persistent Widow, Jesus tells of a widow who persistently petitions an unjust judge until he grants her request. The lesson is to be persistent in prayer and not lose heart.

   - **Significance:** Jesus teaches that God is just and attentive. If an unjust judge can be swayed by persistence, how much more will a loving and just God respond to the persistent prayers of His people.

3. **Humility in Prayer (Luke 18:9-14)** In the Parable of the Pharisee and the Tax Collector, Jesus contrasts the prayers of a self-righteous Pharisee and a humble tax collector. The Pharisee boasts of his righteousness, while the tax collector humbly asks for mercy.

   - **Significance:** Jesus emphasises that humility and a contrite heart are essential in prayer. God values sincere repentance and humility over self-righteousness.

4. **Faith in Prayer (Mark 11:22-24)** Jesus encourages His disciples to have faith in God, assuring them that if they believe, they will receive whatever they ask for in prayer.

   - **Significance:** Jesus highlights the power of faith in prayer, teaching that genuine faith and trust in God's power can result in answered prayers.

5. **Private Prayer (Matthew 6:5-6)** Jesus advises His followers to pray in private rather than seeking public recognition, emphasising that prayer should be a sincere, personal communication with God.
    - o **Significance:** Jesus underscores the importance of authenticity in prayer, teaching that it is not about outward appearances but about a genuine relationship with God.

Jesus' Prayer Life

1. **Jesus Prays in Solitude (Mark 1:35)** Jesus often withdrew to solitary places early in the morning to pray.

    - **Significance:** This highlights Jesus' prioritisation of communion with the Father, setting an example of the importance of seeking solitude and dedicated time for prayer, especially before embarking on ministry activities.

2. **Prayer Before Important Decisions (Luke 6:12-13)** Before selecting His twelve apostles, Jesus spent the entire night in prayer.

    - **Significance:** This underscores the importance of seeking God's guidance and wisdom through prayer before making significant decisions, demonstrating Jesus' dependence on the Father.

3. **Prayer in Times of Distress (Matthew 26:36-46)** In the Garden of Gethsemane, before His arrest, Jesus prays fervently, expressing His anguish and submitting to the Father's will.

    - **Significance:** Jesus' prayer in Gethsemane exemplifies how to seek God's strength and submit to His will in times of intense distress and difficulty, highlighting the human aspect of Jesus' experience and His reliance on the Father.

4. **Intercessory Prayer (John 17)** In John 17, Jesus prays for His disciples and for all future believers, asking for their protection, unity, and sanctification.

    - **Significance:** This prayer demonstrates Jesus' role as an intercessor and His deep concern for His followers. It serves as a model for intercessory prayer, emphasising the importance of praying for others.

5. **Prayer of Thanksgiving (Matthew 11:25-26)** Jesus offers a prayer of thanksgiving to the Father, praising Him for revealing truths to the humble and not to the wise and learned.

    - **Significance:** Jesus' example of giving thanks in prayer highlights the importance of gratitude and recognising God's sovereignty in revealing His truth.

By studying Jesus' teachings on prayer and His own prayer life, we can learn valuable lessons on how to cultivate a deep, sincere, and effective prayer practice. Jesus' example encourages us to approach God with humility, persistence, faith, and a heart aligned with His will.

Old and New Testament Miracles and Testimonies: The Power of Prayer

Throughout history, countless stories and testimonies highlight the miraculous power of prayer and God's faithfulness in responding to His people's petitions. Here are a few significant biblical examples that illustrate the transformative impact of prayer, showcasing how God intervenes in miraculous ways.

Old Testament Miracles and Testimonies

Hannah's Prayer for a Child (1 Samuel 1:9-20)

Story: Hannah, who was barren, fervently prayed for a son, promising to dedicate him to the Lord's service. God answered her prayer, and she gave birth to Samuel, who became a great prophet.

Miracle: The birth of Samuel to a previously barren woman.

Testimony: This story underscores the importance of persistent and heartfelt prayer and God's ability to grant even the deepest desires of our hearts.

Elijah and the Prophets of Baal (1 Kings 18:20-39)

Story: Elijah challenged the prophets of Baal to a contest to demonstrate the power of the true God. He prayed for God to send fire from heaven to consume his offering, and God responded powerfully.

Miracle: Fire from heaven consumed Elijah's offering, proving God's supremacy.

Testimony: This event illustrates God's willingness to reveal His power in response to the prayers of His faithful servants.

Hezekiah's Healing (2 Kings 20:1-11)

Story: King Hezekiah was terminally ill and prayed fervently for healing. God heard his prayer and granted him 15 more years of life.

Miracle: Hezekiah's recovery from a fatal illness.

Testimony: This account demonstrates God's compassion and power to heal in response to sincere prayer.

New Testament Miracles and Testimonies

Jesus Feeds the 5,000 (Matthew 14:13-21)

Story: Faced with a large, hungry crowd, Jesus prayed over five loaves and two fish, which then miraculously multiplied to feed over 5,000 people.

Miracle: The multiplication of food to feed thousands.

Testimony: This miracle shows Jesus' ability to meet physical needs and the power of prayer in providing abundantly.

Healing of the Blind Man (John 9:1-12)

Story: Jesus healed a man born blind by praying and applying mud to his eyes, restoring his sight.

Miracle: The restoration of sight to a man born blind.

Testimony: This healing highlights Jesus' power over physical ailments and the transformative effect of prayer and faith.

Peter's Release from Prison (Acts 12:1-17)

Story: Peter was imprisoned by King Herod, and the church fervently prayed for his release. An angel appeared, freed Peter, and led him out of the prison.

Miracle: Peter's miraculous escape from prison.

Testimony: This event underscores the power of communal prayer and God's ability to intervene in seemingly impossible situations.

Conclusion

The stories and testimonies of answered prayers and miracles, powerfully illustrate the faithfulness and responsiveness of God. These accounts encourage believers to approach God with faith and persistence, trusting in His ability to intervene in miraculous ways.

As you read these accounts, remember that the same God who performed these miracles and answered these prayers is active today. Expect miracles in your life and believe in the power of your prayers. Share your own testimonies of God's intervention with others to encourage and inspire faith. Your story might be the beacon of hope someone else needs to trust in the power of prayer.

Understanding the Holy Spirit

Introduction to the Holy Spirit

The Holy Spirit is the third person of the Trinity, alongside God the Father and God the Son, Jesus Christ. He is not an impersonal force or abstract power, but a living, personal being who plays a vital role in the life of every believer. Understanding the Holy Spirit is essential for living a fruitful Christian life because He is the one who empowers, guides, and sustains us in our journey of faith.

The Purpose of the Holy Spirit

The primary purpose of the Holy Spirit is to glorify Jesus Christ and to work in the hearts of believers to transform them into the likeness of Christ. The Holy Spirit has several key roles, each essential to our spiritual growth and effectiveness as followers of Christ.

1. **The Holy Spirit as a Helper and Advocate**
    - Jesus promised that the Holy Spirit would be our Helper and Advocate. In John 14:16-17, Jesus says, "And I will ask the Father, and He will give you another Helper, to be with you forever, even the Spirit of truth, whom the world cannot receive because it neither sees Him nor knows Him. You know Him, for He dwells with you and will be in you."

- The Holy Spirit advocates on our behalf, guiding us into all truth and helping us to live in a way that honours God.

2. **The Holy Spirit as a Teacher**

    - The Holy Spirit teaches us and helps us understand the deep truths of God's Word. In John 14:26, Jesus said, "But the Helper, the Holy Spirit, whom the Father will send in My name, He will teach you all things and bring to your remembrance all that I have said to you."

    - Through the Holy Spirit, we gain spiritual wisdom and insight, which enables us to grow in our understanding of God's Word and His will for our lives.

3. **The Holy Spirit as a Source of Power**

    - The Holy Spirit empowers believers to live out their faith and to fulfil the Great Commission. Acts 1:8 declares, "But you will receive power when the Holy Spirit has come upon you, and you will be My witnesses in Jerusalem and in all Judea and Samaria, and to the end of the earth."

    - This power is essential for witnessing, performing spiritual gifts, and living a victorious Christian life.

4. **The Holy Spirit as a Comforter and Counsellor**

    - In times of trouble, the Holy Spirit brings comfort and peace to our hearts. Romans 8:26-27 says, "Likewise, the Spirit helps us in our weakness. For we do not know what to pray for as we ought, but the Spirit Himself intercedes for us with groanings too deep for words. And He who searches hearts knows what is the mind of the Spirit, because the Spirit intercedes for the saints according to the will of God."

- o The Holy Spirit is our divine Counsellor, guiding us through life's challenges and comforting us in times of sorrow.

5. **The Holy Spirit as a Source of Spiritual Gifts and Fruit**

    - o The Holy Spirit bestows spiritual gifts upon believers for the edification of the Church (1 Corinthians 12:4-11). These gifts enable us to serve one another and to build up the body of Christ.

    - o Additionally, the Holy Spirit produces the fruit of the Spirit in our lives, which are characteristics of a life transformed by God. Galatians 5:22-23 lists these fruits as "love, joy, peace, patience, kindness, goodness, faithfulness, gentleness, and self-control."

The Importance of the Holy Spirit in a Believer's Life

The Holy Spirit is essential for every aspect of a believer's life. Without the Holy Spirit, we cannot live the Christian life as God intends. Here are some reasons why the Holy Spirit is vital:

1. **The Holy Spirit Guides Us into Truth**

    - Jesus said in John 16:13, "When the Spirit of truth comes, He will guide you into all the truth, for He will not speak on His own authority, but whatever He hears He will speak, and He will declare to you the things that are to come."
    - The Holy Spirit helps us discern truth from falsehood, leading us on the path of righteousness.

2. **The Holy Spirit Convicts Us of Sin**

    - John 16:8 says, "And when He comes, He will convict the world concerning sin and righteousness and judgment."
    - The Holy Spirit works in our hearts to make us aware of our sins, leading us to repentance and a deeper relationship with God.

3. **The Holy Spirit Seals Us for Salvation**

    - Ephesians 1:13-14 states, "In Him you also, when you heard the word of truth, the gospel of your salvation, and believed in Him, were sealed with the promised Holy Spirit, who is the guarantee of our inheritance until we acquire possession of it, to the praise of His glory."

- The Holy Spirit is the seal and guarantee of our salvation, assuring us of our eternal inheritance in Christ.

4. **The Holy Spirit Enables Us to Pray**

    - Romans 8:26 explains, "Likewise, the Spirit helps us in our weakness. For we do not know what to pray for as we ought, but the Spirit Himself intercedes for us with groanings too deep for words."

    - The Holy Spirit intercedes for us, especially when we are unsure of what to pray, aligning our prayers with the will of God.

5. **The Holy Spirit Produces Holiness in Us**

    - The Holy Spirit sanctifies us, making us more like Christ. 2 Thessalonians 2:13 says, "But we ought always to give thanks to God for you, brothers beloved by the Lord, because God chose you as the first fruits to be saved, through sanctification by the Spirit and belief in the truth."

    - Through the work of the Holy Spirit, we grow in holiness and become conformed to the image of Christ.

The Role of the Holy Spirit in Prayer

The Holy Spirit plays a crucial role in our prayer life. He not only helps us to pray but also empowers our prayers, making them effective and aligned with God's will. When we invite the Holy Spirit into our prayers, we are inviting God's presence and power to work in our lives.

1. **The Holy Spirit Helps Us Pray According to God's Will**
    - Romans 8:27 says, "And He who searches hearts knows what is the mind of the Spirit, because the Spirit intercedes for the saints according to the will of God."
    - The Holy Spirit ensures that our prayers are in line with God's perfect will, leading to answered prayers.

2. **The Holy Spirit Gives Us Boldness in Prayer**
    - Ephesians 3:16-17a, 20 says, "I pray that out of His glorious riches He may strengthen you with power through His Spirit in your inner being, so that Christ may dwell in your hearts through faith... Now to Him who is able to do immeasurably more than all we ask or imagine, according to His power that is at work within us."
    - Through the Holy Spirit, we can approach God's throne of grace with confidence, knowing that He is able to do far more than we can ask or imagine.

3. **The Holy Spirit Reminds Us of God's Promises**
    - In John 14:26, Jesus said, "But the Helper, the Holy Spirit, whom the Father will send in My name, He will teach you all things and bring to your remembrance all that I have said to you."
    - The Holy Spirit brings to mind the promises of God, giving us faith and assurance as we pray.

A Prayer to Invite the Holy Spirit

Our Dear Heavenly Father,

I thank You for the precious gift of Your Holy Spirit. I acknowledge that without Him, I am powerless and unable to live the life You have called me to. I invite the Holy Spirit to come and fill my heart today.

Holy Spirit, I welcome You into every area of my life. Guide me into all truth and reveal to me the depths of God's Word. Empower me to live boldly for Christ and to fulfil the purpose that You have set before me. Comfort me in times of trouble and strengthen me in times of weakness. Produce in me the fruit of the Spirit, so that my life may be a testimony of Your transforming power.

As I pray, intercede for me, aligning my prayers with the will of God. Help me to pray with faith, knowing that You are with me, and that You hear me. I surrender all that I am to You and ask that You would lead me in the way everlasting.

Thank You, Holy Spirit, for Your constant presence and for the work You are doing in me. I trust in Your guidance and rely on Your strength each day.

In Jesus' Precious Name, I Pray.

Amen.

The Power of Intercession

What is Intercession?

Intercession is a special form of prayer where we advocate for others, lifting up their needs, concerns, and struggles to God. It's about seeking His intervention and grace on their behalf. While the prayers in this book guide you through your personal challenges, intercession encourages us to extend our prayers outward, focusing on the needs of those around us.

Why Intercede?

Interceding for others is a profound expression of love and compassion. It reflects a deep concern for the well-being of others and a willingness to engage in spiritual support on their behalf. The Bible offers powerful examples of intercessors who made a significant impact through their prayers. For instance, Moses interceded for the Israelites (Exodus 32:11-14), and Jesus continues to intercede for us as our high priest (Hebrews 7:25).

How to Incorporate Intercession

You can use the prayers in this book as a foundation for interceding on behalf of others. Here's how to make your intercession more effective:

Identify Needs: Reflect on those in your life facing challenges—family members, friends, colleagues, or even broader community or global issues.

Pray Specifically: Personalise each prayer by inserting the names and specific struggles of those you are praying for. For example, instead of a general prayer, you might say, "Lord, I lift up [Name] who is facing [specific issue]." This personal touch adds depth and sincerity to your intercessions.

Pray with Faith: Approach your intercession with confidence in God's ability to hear and answer prayers. Remember, intercession involves trusting in His perfect plan and timing, not merely asking for changes in circumstances.

Follow Up: Keep track of the prayers you've lifted up and look for opportunities to offer encouragement and support. Your ongoing concern and prayers can bring comfort and hope to those you are praying for.

In this book, you'll find 34 heartfelt prayers designed to support you through everyday struggles and challenges. Each prayer offers comfort, guidance, and strength. Recognise, too, the powerful role of intercession. By extending your prayers to others, you not only seek God's grace for them but also deepen your own spiritual journey.

Customising these prayers for others enhances their impact. Personalise your intercessions by adding names and specific situations, showing genuine care and concern.

Interceding for others is about standing with those in need and believing in the transformative power of prayer. As you seek strength and solace for yourself, remember that your prayers can also make a meaningful difference in others' lives. Embrace this opportunity to support those you care about and witness the powerful work of God's grace and love.

The Prayer of Jabez

1 Chronicles 4:10:

"Jabez cried out to the God of Israel, saying, 'Oh, that You would bless me indeed and enlarge my territory, that Your hand would be with me, and that You would keep me from evil, that I may not cause pain!' So God granted him what he requested."

The Prayer of Jabez is a profound yet straightforward prayer that can significantly impact your daily life. It consists of four simple steps that encompass key aspects of spiritual growth, divine favour, guidance, and protection. Let's delve into each step and understand how incorporating them into your daily prayers can bring about transformative changes. By praying the Prayer of Jabez daily, you align yourself with God's will, inviting His blessings, guidance, and protection into your life

Here's a more detailed unpacking of the Prayer of Jabez with practical applications for everyday life:

"Oh, that You would bless me indeed"

This is a request for God's abundant blessings in all aspects of life. It goes beyond asking for basic needs, expressing a desire for God's extraordinary favour and provision. Trust in His ability to provide beyond your expectations.

"Enlarge my territory"

This is a plea for God to expand your influence, opportunities, and impact. It's about stepping into new areas, meeting new people, and taking on greater responsibilities. Pray for the courage to take on new challenges and the ability to see and seize opportunities for growth.

"That Your hand would be with me"

This is a request for God's guidance, presence, and support in all endeavours. It acknowledges that true success and protection come from God. Recognise that you cannot achieve your goals without God's help and presence.

"That You would keep me from evil"

This is a plea for protection from harm, temptation, and negative influences. It's about seeking God's safeguarding from anything that could cause physical, spiritual, or emotional pain. Make this a part of your daily prayers to cover yourself with God's protection.

Daily Prayer Inspired by the Prayer of Jabez

Our Dear Heavenly Father,

I come before You with a humble heart, seeking Your presence and guidance in my life. Oh, that You would bless me indeed, showering me with Your abundant grace, wisdom, and provision. Fill my life with Your blessings, Lord, in ways that surpass my understanding.

Enlarge my territory, Father. Open doors of opportunity and bring the right people into my life who can support and uplift me. Help me to grow in my career, personal relationships, and spiritual journey. Grant me the courage to step into new challenges and the wisdom to navigate them successfully.

Let Your hand be with me, Lord. Guide my every decision and action. I cannot do this without You. Walk with me daily, leading me on the path You have prepared for me. May I always be aware of Your presence and rely on Your strength.

Keep me from evil, I pray. Protect me from harm, negative influences, and spiritual attacks. Surround me with Your divine protection, shielding me from anything that could cause me pain or lead me astray. Keep my heart pure and my mind focused on You.

Thank You, Father, for hearing my prayer and for Your unfailing love and faithfulness. I trust in Your perfect plan for my life and rest in the assurance that You are with me always.

In Jesus' precious name I pray,

Amen.

The Ten Commandments:

A Guide for Living

Introduction:
The Ten Commandments are timeless principles given by God to guide our relationship with Him and with others. They are foundational to living a life aligned with His will and reflecting His character. As you seek to grow in faith and embody the Fruit of the Spirit, these commandments can serve as a moral compass and a reminder of the core values God desires for us.

The Ten Commandments:

1. *You shall have no other gods before Me.*

Verse: Exodus 20:3
God demands exclusive devotion and worship. He is the only true God, and no other gods should be worshipped or placed above Him.

2. *You shall not make for yourself a carved image—or any likeness of anything that is in heaven above, or on the earth below, or in the water beneath the earth. You shall not bow down to them or serve them.*

Verse: Exodus 20:4-5
This commandment forbids the creation and worship of idols or images. It emphasises worshiping God in spirit and truth, without physical representations.

3. *You shall not take the name of the Lord your God in vain.*

Verse: Exodus 20:7
This commandment warns against misusing or disrespecting God's name. It calls for reverence and respect in how we speak about God.

4. *Remember the Sabbath day, to keep it holy. Six days you shall labour and do all your work, but the seventh day is the Sabbath of the Lord your God. In it you shall do no work.*

Verse: Exodus 20:8-10
The Sabbath is a day of rest and spiritual reflection. It honours God's creation and provides time for renewal and worship.

5. *Honour your father and your mother, that your days may be long upon the land which the Lord your God is giving you.*

Verse: Exodus 20:12
This commandment emphasises the importance of respecting and valuing parents. It promises blessings and longevity as a result of honouring family.

6. *You shall not murder.*

Verse: Exodus 20:13
This commandment prohibits the unlawful taking of another's life. It underscores the sanctity of human life and the importance of peace.

7. *You shall not commit adultery.*

Verse: Exodus 20:14

This commandment forbids marital infidelity. It upholds the sanctity of marriage and fidelity within the relationship.

> 8. *You shall not steal.*

Verse: Exodus 20:15

This commandment prohibits taking what does not belong to you. It promotes respect for others' property and honesty.

> 9. *You shall not bear false witness against your neighbour.*

Verse: Exodus 20:16

This commandment forbids giving false testimony or lying. It emphasises truthfulness and integrity in all communications.

> 10. *You shall not covet your neighbour's house; you shall not covet your neighbour's wife, nor his male servant, nor his female servant, nor his ox, nor his donkey, nor anything that is your neighbour's.*

Verse: Exodus 20:17

This commandment addresses the desire for what belongs to others. It promotes contentment and discourages envy or greed.

Reflection and Application:

Each of these commandments calls us to live in a way that honours God and fosters healthy relationships with others. As you read and meditate on these principles, ask the Holy Spirit to guide you in applying them to your daily life. Seek to embody the values they represent and allow them to shape your actions and decisions.

Pray:
Lord, thank You for the wisdom and guidance found in Your Ten Commandments. Help me to live according to these principles, honouring You in all that I do. May these commandments be a constant reminder of Your love and truth, guiding my actions and interactions with others. Empower me to follow Your ways, reflecting Your character in my life.

In Jesus' Mighty Name,
Amen.

Prayer of Salvation

Word Encouragement

Dear Friend,

I want to encourage you today as you take this step of faith. God's love for you is immense and unchanging. No matter your past or the mistakes you've made, His grace is sufficient for you. As you invite Jesus into your heart, know that you are a new creation in Christ. The journey ahead is filled with His presence, guidance, and abundant love. Trust in His promises, lean on His strength, and walk in the freedom and joy that comes from knowing Him. Remember, you are never alone—God is always with you, ready to lead you and fill your life with His peace and purpose.

Be blessed and encouraged as you walk with Him.

With love and prayers.

Prayer of Salvation

Our Dear Heavenly Father,

I come before you acknowledging my need for your forgiveness and grace. Your Word tells me in Romans 3:23 that "all have sinned and fall short of the glory of God." I confess that I have sinned against you, and I am truly sorry. Please forgive me, as 1 John 1:9 assures me that "if we confess our sins, he is faithful and just and will forgive us our sins and purify us from all unrighteousness."

Lord Jesus, I believe in your sacrifice for me. Your Word in Romans 5:8 declares that "God demonstrates his own love for us in this: While we were still sinners, Christ died for us." I accept your gift of salvation and believe that you died on the cross for my sins, as Romans 10:9 promises that "if you declare with your mouth, 'Jesus is Lord,' and believe in your heart that God raised him from the dead, you will be saved."

I invite you into my heart and life, Lord Jesus, to be my Savior and Lord. Your Word says in John 1:12 that "to all who did receive him, to those who believed in his name, he gave the right to become children of God." I receive you now and ask that you come into my life, cleanse me, and guide me by your Holy Spirit.

Thank you, Father, for your mercy and grace. Your Word assures me in Ephesians 2:8-9 that "it is by grace you have been saved, through faith—and this is not from yourselves, it is the gift of God—not by works, so that no one can boast." I place my trust in you and commit to following you all the days of my life.

In Jesus' precious name, I pray.
Amen.

Verse

1 John 1:9

"If we confess our sins, he is faithful and just and will forgive us our sins and purify us from all unrighteousness."

✱✱✱

Embrace God's grace, confess your sins, and accept Jesus as your Saviour—experience the transformation of becoming a new creation in Christ, walking in His love, peace, and purpose forevermore.

Daily Reflection

Prayer over Anointing Oil

As you take a simple bottle of olive oil from your pantry to use for anointing, remember that it's not the oil itself, but your faith and God's power that make this act sacred. Olive oil has been used throughout the Bible as a symbol of the Holy Spirit's presence and blessing.

By anointing with this oil, you are inviting God's protection, healing, and guidance into your life. Trust that God will honour your faith and meet you in this moment, bringing His peace, comfort, and strength to whatever you face.

Blessings to you.

Word Encouragement

Dear Beloved,

As you prepare to anoint yourself, your loved ones, your home, and the aspects of your life that you hold dear, know that you are engaging in a powerful act of faith and trust in God. Anointing with oil is a sacred tradition, deeply rooted in Scripture, symbolising the presence, blessing, and power of the Holy Spirit.

Remember that as you anoint, you are invoking God's protection, healing, and divine intervention. Just as David was anointed and empowered by the Holy Spirit, and just as Jesus' disciples anointed the sick and saw them healed, you too are participating in a holy act that invites God's miraculous touch into your life.

Take heart and be encouraged by Psalm 23:5-6, which assures us of God's overflowing blessings and his constant presence: "You anoint my head with oil; my cup overflows. Surely your goodness and love will follow me all the days of my life, and I will dwell in the house of the Lord forever." Let this promise fill you with confidence and peace as you perform this anointing.

Know that God is with you in every step you take. He hears your prayers, sees your heart, and is ready to pour out His blessings upon you. Trust in His goodness, lean on His strength, and expect His miracles. May this act of anointing be a profound experience of His love, grace, and power in your life.

In faith and with God's blessings.

Prayer over Anointing Oil

Our Dear Heavenly Father,

I come before You today with a heart full of hope and trust. As I hold this oil, I seek Your divine blessing upon it, asking that it be sanctified and filled with Your Holy Spirit. Your Word in James 5:14 instructs us, "Is anyone among you sick? Let them call the elders of the church to pray over them and anoint them with oil in the name of the Lord." Bless this oil for healing and restoration.

Lord, as Your Spirit came upon David when he was anointed with oil (1 Samuel 16:13), let Your Spirit be present in this oil, bringing healing, comfort, and divine intervention. Just as Jesus sent out His disciples to anoint the sick with oil and heal them (Mark 6:13), I claim that same authority and power in Jesus' name.

Your Word declares in Isaiah 61:1, "The Spirit of the Sovereign Lord is on me, because the Lord has anointed me to proclaim good news to the poor. He has sent me to bind up the broken-hearted, to proclaim freedom for the captives and release from darkness for the prisoners." May this oil proclaim good news, bring healing, freedom, and light.

In Psalm 23:5, your word says, "You anoint my head with oil; my cup overflows." Let this oil be a symbol of Your overflowing blessings in my life, bringing peace, comfort, and hope.

Lord, as I anoint myself with this oil, I pray for Your strength to face daily challenges, for your peace that surpasses all understanding and Your wisdom to guide my decisions. Help me to trust in You with all my heart.

Lord, I thank You for my home. As I anoint my house, I pray for Your protection over every room. May it be a sanctuary of peace, love, and harmony.

Father, I lift up my children to You. As I anoint them, I ask for Your guidance, protection, and blessings upon their lives. Let them grow in wisdom and favour with God and man.

Lord, I pray for Your protection over our vehicles. Safeguard us from accidents and harm and let may your angels encamp around us.

Father, I commit our finances into Your hands. I pray for Your provision and blessing.

Lord, I lift up my spouse to You. As I anoint them, I ask for Your love, unity, and strength in our relationship. Let our marriage reflect Christ's love for the church.

Thank You, Lord, for loving me unconditionally. Let this oil be a conduit for Your miraculous works, bringing wholeness to our bodies, minds, and spirits.

In Jesus' mighty name, I pray.

Amen.

Verse

Psalm 23:5-6 (NIV)

"You prepare a table before me in the presence of my enemies. You anoint my head with oil, my cup overflows. Surely your goodness and love will follow me all the days of my life, and I will dwell in the house of the Lord forever."

✶✶✶

Anointing with oil is a sacred act, inviting God's presence and power to bring healing, protection, and divine favour into our lives.

Daily Reflection

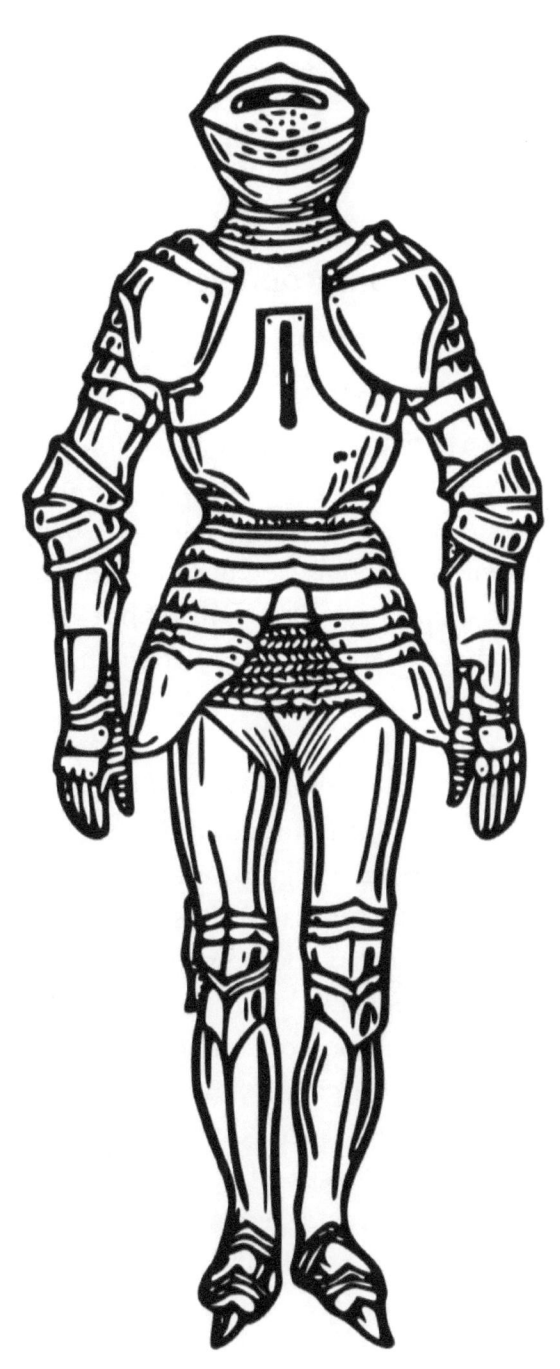

Prayer to Wear the Full Armour of God

Word Encouragement

Dear Friend,

As you prepare to pray and put on the armour of God, I want to encourage you with this truth: you are not alone in the battles you face. The Lord, your mighty protector, stands with you, equipping you with everything you need to face each challenge. The armour of God is not just a metaphor but a powerful spiritual reality that covers you in His strength, His truth, and His peace.

When you fasten the belt of truth, know that you are grounded in the unchanging truth of God's Word. It will guide your steps and guard your heart against the lies of the enemy. As you put on the breastplate of righteousness, remember that you are covered in the righteousness of Christ, protecting your heart from anything that would try to lead you astray.

As you prepare your feet with the gospel of peace, be confident that wherever you go, you carry the peace of Christ with you—a peace that surpasses all understanding. When you take up the shield of faith, know that your faith is a powerful defence against all the attacks of the enemy. The helmet of salvation will guard your mind, reminding you of the hope and security you have in Jesus. Finally, the sword of the Spirit, which is the Word of God, is your weapon of victory—use it to declare His promises over your life.

Remember, the struggles you face are not just physical; they are spiritual. But with God's armour, you are fully equipped to stand firm and overcome. As you pray and put on this armour each day, trust that God is with you, empowering you to face every trial with courage and confidence.

Here's a quick reference to the scriptures for each piece of the armour:
- **Belt of Truth:** Ephesians 6:14
- **Breastplate of Righteousness:** Ephesians 6:14
- **Gospel of Peace:** Ephesians 6:15
- **Shield of Faith:** Ephesians 6:16
- **Helmet of Salvation:** Ephesians 6:17
- **Sword of the Spirit:** Ephesians 6:17

Take heart, my friend. You are covered, protected, and loved by the Almighty God. As you pray, believe that He is working in your life, guiding you, strengthening you, and giving you victory in every situation.

With faith and courage.

Prayer to Wear the Full Armour of God

Our Dear Heavenly Father,

I come before You today, humbly seeking Your strength and protection as I prepare to face the challenges of this day. I know that the battles I encounter are not merely physical but spiritual, and I need Your armour to stand firm. Lord, I put on the full armour of God, as Your Word instructs, trusting in Your power to shield me from all harm.

I fasten the **belt of truth** around my waist, grounding myself in Your Word (Ephesians 6:14). Let Your truth guide my every step, protecting me from the lies and deceptions of the enemy. May I walk in honesty and integrity, standing firm in the knowledge that Your Word is a lamp to my feet and a light to my path (Psalm 119:105).

I place on the **breastplate of righteousness**, knowing that I am covered by the righteousness of Christ (Ephesians 6:14). Guard my heart, Lord, from anything that seeks to lead me away from Your will. Help me to live a life that is pleasing to You, reflecting Your love and grace in all I do.

I prepare my feet with the **gospel of peace** (Ephesians 6:15). Wherever I go today, may I carry Your peace with me—a peace that surpasses all understanding (Philippians 4:7). Let me be a peacemaker, bringing calm and comfort to those around me, and standing firm in the assurance that You are with me.

I take up the **shield of faith**, trusting that it will extinguish all the flaming arrows of the evil one (Ephesians 6:16). Strengthen my faith, Lord, so that I can resist every attack and stand firm in the face of adversity. When doubts and fears arise, help me to trust in Your unfailing love and power.

I put on the **helmet of salvation**, guarding my mind and thoughts with the hope and assurance I have in You (Ephesians

6:17). Protect me from the enemy's attempts to plant seeds of doubt and fear. Remind me daily that my salvation is secure in Christ, and that nothing can separate me from Your love (Romans 8:38-39).

Finally, I take up the **sword of the Spirit**, which is Your Word (Ephesians 6:17). Let Your Word be alive and active in my heart, sharper than any double-edged sword (Hebrews 4:12). Empower me to declare Your promises over my life and to use Your Word to stand against the enemy's schemes.

Lord, as I put on this full armour, I trust in Your protection and guidance. I know that You are with me, fighting my battles and leading me through every challenge. I stand firm in Your strength, confident that no weapon formed against me shall prosper (Isaiah 54:17).

I commit to praying this prayer every day, knowing that Your armour is not just words but a powerful spiritual reality that equips me to face the world with courage, peace, and victory. Thank You, Lord, for Your unending love, for always being by my side, and for empowering me to overcome every obstacle through Your mighty power.

In the powerful name of Jesus, I pray,

Amen.

Verse

Ephesians 6:11 (NIV):

> *"Put on the full armour of God, so that you can take your stand against the devil's schemes."*

✯✯✯

When you put on the full armour of God each day, you prepare yourself with divine protection and strength to face the world's challenges with unwavering faith and courage.

Daily Reflection

Prayer for Unwavering Faith

Word Encouragement

Dear Friend,

As you pray this prayer, remember that faith is the cornerstone of your relationship with God. Just as Hebrews 11:1 reminds us, faith is the assurance of things hoped for and the conviction of things not seen. Trust in God's promises, knowing that He is always with you, guiding and sustaining you through every challenge.

When doubt begins to creep in, hold tightly to the truth that "I can do all things through Christ who strengthens me" (Philippians 4:13). Your faith, no matter how small it may seem, has the power to move mountains. Immerse yourself in God's Word, meditate on His promises, and allow His Holy Spirit to fill you with unwavering confidence.

Anoint yourself and your loved ones with oil, symbolising the Holy Spirit's presence and power in your life. Believe that God is working mightily on your behalf, breaking chains, and setting you free from every generational curse.

May your faith deepen with each passing day, and may you experience the abundant life that Jesus promised. Stand firm, for God is faithful, and He will never leave you nor forsake you.

In His love and grace.

Prayer for Unwavering Faith

Our Dear Heavenly Father,

I come before You with a humble heart, seeking to build an unwavering faith and deepen my relationship with You. Your Word tells me, "Without faith, it is impossible to please God, because anyone who comes to Him must believe that He exists and that He rewards those who earnestly seek Him" (Hebrews 11:6). Lord, I earnestly seek You today, longing for a faith that stands firm and unshaken in the face of life's challenges.

Father, I pray as the apostles did, "Increase our faith!" (Luke 17:5). I acknowledge that faith comes from hearing the message, and the message is heard through the word about Christ (Romans 10:17). Help me to immerse myself in Your Word, to meditate on Your promises, and to trust in Your unfailing love and faithfulness. Your Word assures me, "I can do all things through Christ who strengthens me" (Philippians 4:13). Strengthen my faith, Lord, so that I may face every trial with confidence, knowing that Your power sustains me. Help me to live by the truth that "The righteous will live by faith" (Habakkuk 2:4) and that my faith serves as a shield against all the attacks of the evil one (Ephesians 6:16).

Lord, I confess any doubt or unbelief that may be hindering my faith. I echo the prayer of the man in the gospel who said, "I do believe; help me overcome my unbelief!" (Mark 9:24). Forgive me for the times I have allowed fear and doubt to overshadow my trust in You. Fill me with Your Holy Spirit and grant me the assurance of things hoped for and the conviction of things not seen (Hebrews 11:1). Your Word promises that "If you have faith as small as a mustard seed, you can say to this mountain, 'Move from here to there,' and it will move. Nothing will be impossible for you" (Matthew 17:20). Lord, even a small, unwavering faith can accomplish great things through You. Help me to step out in faith, trusting that You are always with me and will never leave me nor forsake me (Deuteronomy 31:6).

Father, I thank You for Your faithfulness and for the ways You have worked in my life. May my faith remain steadfast, serving as a testimony to others of Your goodness and power. Let my life reflect the truth of Your Word, that others may see my unwavering faith and glorify You in heaven. I come boldly before Your throne, standing on Your promises. Your Word says in Matthew 21:22, "And whatever you ask in prayer, you will receive, if you have faith." Today, Father, I ask You to help me grow daily in unwavering faith. Help me to trust fully in Your control and to know without doubt that I can rely on You completely.

Even when I face difficult situations, help me to remember that You are with me. Keep my faith steady, even when trials come my way. Sometimes, Lord, I struggle to understand Your plan, and the path ahead seems dark; help me to see Your light and to trust that You are guiding me. Today, I ask You to strengthen my faith and my walk with You. Help me to focus on You, to draw nearer to You, and to rest in the assurance that You will never leave me or forsake me. Lord, I know that it is my unwavering faith in You that will carry me through. Give me the ability to see You, hear You, and trust You with all my heart.

Father, even when I cannot see it, I trust that You are working. Guard my heart against doubt and unbelief. Today, I ask You for hope, faith, peace, and strength. Be with me in every season of my life. Help me to trust what I cannot see, knowing that You are the author, perfecter, and source of my faith. Lord, I place my trust in You unconditionally, surrendering my life, decisions, and future into Your hands.

I ask all this in Jesus' Precious Name,
Amen.

Verse

Hebrews 11:1

"Now faith is confidence in what we hope for and assurance about what we do not see."

✱✱✱

Deepen your faith, trust in God's promises, and walk confidently in His love and strength.

Daily Reflection

Prayer for Myself

Word Encouragement

Dear Friend,

As you lift your heart in prayer for yourself, know that you are seen and deeply loved by the Creator of the universe. Whatever challenges you may be facing, God is with you in the midst of it all. Psalm 46:1 assures us, "God is our refuge and strength, an ever-present help in trouble." You are not alone; He is walking alongside you through every trial.

Your decision to pray for yourself is a powerful testament to your faith and trust in God's provision. Philippians 4:19 reminds us, "And my God will meet all your needs according to the riches of his glory in Christ Jesus." Trust in His promise to provide for you abundantly, both spiritually and practically.

In moments of doubt or fear, hold fast to the truth of Isaiah 41:10: "So do not fear, for I am with you; do not be dismayed, for I am your God. I will strengthen you and help you; I will uphold you with my righteous right hand." Allow these words to strengthen your faith and uplift your spirit.

As you pray, pour out your heart honestly and openly before God. He already knows your needs, but He delights in hearing from His children. Psalm 34:17-18 assures us, "The righteous cry out, and the Lord hears them; he delivers them from all their troubles. The Lord is close to the broken-hearted and saves those who are crushed in spirit." Let these words bring you comfort and assurance.

May your time of prayer be a sacred moment of connection

with God, where you experience His peace that surpasses all understanding (Philippians 4:7). Know that He is working in ways that you cannot see.

As you prepare to pray, remember to use the anointing oil as a symbol of your faith and dedication to God's promises. Anoint yourself, your home, and your loved ones, trusting in God's power to bring healing, protection, and favour.

Hold onto hope, dear friend, knowing that God is faithful and His love for you is everlasting. Keep praying, keep trusting, and keep believing in His promises.

With heartfelt encouragement.

Prayer for Myself

Our Dear Heavenly Father,

I humbly come before You today with a heart full of gratitude. Thank You, Lord, for the very breath of life. Your Word is a lamp to my feet and a light to my path (Psalm 119:105). Guide me today and always, that I may walk in Your ways and find peace in Your presence.

Lord, Your Word says, "I can do all things through Christ who strengthens me" (Philippians 4:13). Grant me the strength to face any challenges that come my way, and help me to remember that with You, nothing is impossible.

Father, Your promise in Jeremiah 29:11 reassures me: "For I know the plans I have for you, declares the Lord, plans for welfare and not for evil, to give you a future and a hope." I trust in Your perfect plan for my life. Even when I cannot see the way ahead, I have faith that You are leading me towards a future filled with hope.

Today, Lord, I ask You to give me a spirit of humility when I deal with others. Help me to always be grateful for all that I have and to remember that I have gained nothing on my own. As I humble myself before You, I ask that if anything in my life is not of You, let it be destroyed in Jesus' name. Send Your Word and deliver me from all my evil ways.

Lord, teach me to love others as You have loved me (John 13:34). Help me to be patient, kind, and forgiving. Let my actions reflect Your love so that others may see You through me.

Father, I seek Your wisdom in all that I do. As it is written in James 1:5, "If any of you lacks wisdom, you should ask God, who gives generously to all without finding fault, and it will be given to you." Pour out Your wisdom upon me, that I may make decisions that honour You.

Help me learn how to face every storm with confidence. Father, today I lay my burdens at Your feet. Forgive me if I have wronged anyone. Soften my heart, Lord, and help me be slow to speak. Protect me from the pain of this world. I break every generational curse in Jesus' Name. Your Word says that You have plans to prosper me and not to harm me, plans to give me hope and a future. Today, I claim this blessing in Jesus' name.

In times of anxiety and worry, remind me of Your promise in Philippians 4:6-7: "Do not be anxious about anything, but in every situation, by prayer and petition, with thanksgiving, present your requests to God. And the peace of God, which transcends all understanding, will guard your hearts and your minds in Christ Jesus." Fill my heart with Your peace, Lord, and calm my anxious thoughts.

Lord Jesus, I know that I am a sinner. By faith, I gratefully receive Your gift of salvation. I am ready to trust You as my Lord and Savior. Thank You, Lord Jesus, for saving me. I believe You are the Son of God who died on the cross for my sins and rose from the dead on the third day. Thank You for bearing my sins and giving me the gift of eternal life. Come into my heart, Lord Jesus, and be my Savior.

Thank You, Lord, for Your unending grace and mercy. I am grateful for Your presence in my life and for the many blessings You have bestowed upon me. Each day, I ask for Your guidance, protection, and favour. May my life be a testament to Your goodness and faithfulness.

In Jesus Precious Name I Pray,
Amen.

Verse:

Philippians 4:6-7 (NIV)

> *"Do not be anxious about anything, but in every situation, by prayer and petition, with thanksgiving, present your requests to God. And the peace of God, which transcends all understanding, will guard your hearts and your minds in Christ Jesus*
>
> ✶✶✶
>
> *Trust in God's guidance, find strength in His promises, and embrace His peace, knowing He is always with you.*

Daily Reflection

An Everyday Prayer

Word of Encouragement

Dear Friend,

I want to encourage you today to hold on to the promises of God and to trust in His unfailing love and guidance. As you navigate the challenges and joys of each day, remember that God is always with you, offering His wisdom, strength, and peace. His Word assures us that His mercies are new every morning and His faithfulness is great (Lamentations 3:22-23).

When you face difficult decisions or trials, ask God for wisdom, for He gives generously to all who seek Him (James 1:5). Trust in His strength, knowing that you can do all things through Christ who empowers you (Philippians 4:13). Let your light shine before others, reflecting His love and goodness in everything you do (Matthew 5:16).

I encourage you to pray continually, seeking God's presence and guidance in every aspect of your life. As you pray, anoint yourself and your loved ones with oil, a symbol of the Holy Spirit's presence and God's anointing over your lives. This simple act of faith can bring comfort, healing, and a reminder of God's promise to protect and bless you.

May you find peace in knowing that God is your refuge and strength, an ever-present help in times of trouble (Psalm 46:1). Keep pressing forward with a cheerful spirit, even when things don't go as planned, and trust that God's grace is sufficient for every moment.

Be blessed, and may your faith be strengthened as you walk closely with the Lord each day.

In Christ's love.

An Everyday Prayer

Our Dear Heavenly Father,

I come before You today with a grateful heart, thanking You for the gift of another day. As I begin this day, I acknowledge Your presence in my life and seek Your guidance and strength. Thank You, Lord, for the very breath of life, for allowing me to get up this morning, praising and glorifying Your name.

Your Word tells me, "The steadfast love of the Lord never ceases; His mercies never come to an end; they are new every morning; great is Your faithfulness" (Lamentations 3:22-23). I thank You for Your unfailing love and the new mercies You provide each day. Help me to live in the light of Your grace and extend that grace to others.

Father, I ask for Your wisdom to navigate the challenges of today. Your Word says, "If any of you lacks wisdom, let him ask of God, who gives generously to all without reproach, and it will be given to him" (James 1:5). Grant me discernment in my decisions and actions, that I may walk in Your will and purpose.

Lord, I pray for strength and courage to face any trials that may come my way. As Your Word promises, "I can do all things through Christ who strengthens me" (Philippians 4:13). Empower me with Your Holy Spirit, that I may overcome obstacles and remain steadfast in my faith.

Help me to be a light in this world, reflecting Your love and kindness to those around me. Let my words and actions be a testimony of Your goodness. "Let your light shine before others, that they may see your good deeds and glorify your Father in heaven" (Matthew 5:16). Help me to be compassionate, kind, and loving, and to be a good steward with all that You have blessed me with.

I lift up my loved ones to You, asking for Your protection, provision, and blessings upon them. Surround them with Your love and peace and guide them in their journeys. Protect us all from any evil, harm, or danger. Bless my family and friends as each one of us goes about our daily routines.

Thank You, Lord, for loving me. Even if I fail today and fall short, remind me, Father, that Your mercies are new every morning. Thank You for today, a new opportunity to love, give, and be all that You want me to be. Grant me a cheerful spirit when things don't go my way and give me the strength to keep going even when I am tempted to give up.

I pray for safe travelling mercies and Your blood covering today. Lord, You know our fears and our needs. Give us the strength to face whatever comes our way and the grace to always trust You. Bless us, Lord, and may our cups overflow.

Father, we cannot do life without You. Thank You for being my guiding light.

In Jesus' precious name, I pray,

Amen.

Verse

Proverbs 3:5-6

> *"Trust in the Lord with all your heart and lean not on your own understanding; in all your ways submit to Him, and He will make your paths straight."*

✯✯✯

Trust in God's wisdom and strength each day, walk in His grace, and let His love guide your every step.

Daily Reflection

A Prayer for Overcoming Negativity

Word of Encouragement

Dear Friend,

As you read this prayer, remember that you are never alone. God is with you, shielding you from negativity and filling your life with blessings. Isaiah 54:17 assures us that "no weapon forged against you will prevail, and you will refute every tongue that accuses you." Trust in His protection and know that He transforms every negative word or thought into a blessing for you, as Romans 8:28 says, "And we know that in all things God works for the good of those who love him, who have been called according to his purpose."

Stand strong in your faith, for God's love and grace are greater than any challenge you may face. Keep your heart open to His guidance, and let His peace and strength uplift you. Remember Philippians 4:13: "I can do all this through him who gives me strength." You are cherished and loved beyond measure.

In faith and hope.

A Prayer Against Negativity

Our Dear Heavenly Father,

I come before You, seeking Your protection and peace. When negativity surrounds me and threatens to steal my joy, I ask for Your strength to stand firm. Lord, Your Word in Isaiah 54:17 declares that "no weapon formed against you shall prosper," and I hold onto this promise.

Fill me with Your Holy Spirit, so that I may respond to negativity with grace and love. Help me to remember that my worth and identity are found in You alone. When words or actions of others bring me down, remind me of Psalm 139:14, which says, "I praise you because I am fearfully and wonderfully made; your works are wonderful, I know that full well."

Lord, grant me the wisdom to discern the truth from lies and to focus on Your voice above all others. Philippians 4:8 tells us to think about whatever is true, noble, right, pure, lovely, and admirable. Help me to meditate on these things, keeping my heart and mind in perfect peace.

Forgive those who speak or act against me and soften their hearts with Your love. As Jesus prayed for His persecutors, so I pray for those who bring negativity into my life. May Your light shine through me, overcoming the darkness and bringing healing and reconciliation.

I ask that You turn every negative thought and curse spoken against me into my greatest blessing. Let every harmful word or intent be transformed into a testament of Your power and grace in my life. Romans 8:28 reminds me that "in all things God works for the good of those who love him, who have been called according to his purpose." Use every situation, even the negative ones, for my growth and Your glory.

Lord, be my shield and defender. Surround me with Your angels and let Your peace, which transcends all understanding, guard my heart and mind in Christ Jesus (Philippians 4:7). Thank You for being my refuge and strength, my ever-present help in trouble.

In Jesus' precious name, I pray,

Amen.

Verse

Isaiah 54:17 (KJV)

> *"No weapon that is formed against thee shall prosper; and every tongue that shall rise against thee in judgment thou shalt condemn. This is the heritage of the servants of the Lord, and their righteousness is of me, saith the Lord."*

✲✲✲

> *Embrace God's strength and love, transforming negativity into blessings, and finding peace in His promises.*

Daily Reflection

Prayer for My Children

Word of Encouragement

Dear Friend,

As you pour out your heart in prayer for your children, know that your love and dedication as a parent are deeply cherished by our Heavenly Father. Your commitment to seeking God's protection and guidance over their lives reflects your profound faith and trust in His unfailing love.

Remember the words of Proverbs 22:6, "Train up a child in the way he should go; even when he is old, he will not depart from it." This verse reminds us of the powerful impact of parental guidance rooted in God's wisdom. Your prayers and efforts to instil values of faith, kindness, and humility in your children are shaping their character and future.

Continue to lean on God's promises, knowing that He hears every prayer and holds your children in His loving hands. Trust in His provision, guidance, and protection over their physical, emotional, and spiritual well-being. May your faith be strengthened as you see God's hand at work in their lives.

May God bless you abundantly as you faithfully intercede for your children and lead them in the ways of righteousness. Your role as a parent is a sacred calling, and your prayers are a powerful testament to your love for God and your family.

With heartfelt encouragement and prayers.

Prayer for My Children

Our Dear Heavenly Father,

I come before You with a heart full of love and gratitude for the precious gift of my children. Thank You for blessing me with their lives and entrusting them into my care. Today, I lift them up to You, asking for Your divine protection and guidance over their lives.

Lord, I pray that You cover my children with Your mighty wings (Psalm 91:4). Surround them with Your angels to guard them in all their ways (Psalm 91:11). Keep them safe from all harm and danger, both seen and unseen. Shield them from any evil that may come their way, and let Your presence be their constant protection.

Father, I ask for Your wisdom to fill their hearts and minds (James 1:5). Guide them in every decision they make and help them to walk in Your truth. May they grow in knowledge and understanding, and may their paths be straight and filled with Your blessings.

Lord Jesus, You are the Good Shepherd who lays down His life for the sheep (John 10:11). I pray that You lead my children beside still waters and restore their souls (Psalm 23:2-3). Give them rest and peace in their hearts and help them to trust in You at all times.

Holy Spirit, be their constant companion and guide. Comfort them in times of distress and bring joy to their hearts. Fill them with Your love, joy, peace, patience, kindness, goodness, faithfulness, gentleness, and self-control (Galatians 5:22-23). Help them to grow in character and to reflect Your love in all they do.

Father, I pray for their physical, emotional, and spiritual well-being. Grant them good health, strength, and vitality. Protect their minds from negative influences and fill their hearts with Your love and truth. May they always know that they are deeply loved and valued by You and by their family.

Lord, I ask for Your protection, love, and guidance over each one. Let them know Your goodness, provision, and protection. Guard them against any plots that are meant to harm or bring ruin to them. May they become people of great character. May they develop a real love and care for others. Give them an abundance of kindness and humility.

Lord, as I lift my dear children to You, I ask You to give me, as the parent, the strength, wisdom, guidance, and grace to raise them up to know You, to serve You, and to love You. Help me to live in such a way that my children know my love for them and see Jesus in me. Help us to strengthen our bond and do things together.

I pray that they will be found in Your favour and in the Favor of every person they come into contact with. Through Your love, help them to be a good example to others and to live in a way that honours You.

Help me to put my faith and trust in You as You raise them to be mighty warriors for You.

Thank You, Lord, for hearing my prayers. I trust in Your unfailing love and protection over my children. May they grow to be strong, faithful, and loving individuals who honour You in all they do.

In Jesus' precious name, I pray,
Amen.

Verse

Proverbs 22:6 (ESV)

> *"Train up a child in the way he should go; even when he is old, he will not depart from it."*

✯✯✯

Entrust your children to God's loving care, knowing He will guide and protect them as you nurture their faith and character with unwavering love.

Daily Reflection

Prayer for Healing

Word of Encouragement

Dear Friend,

In times of illness and uncertainty, it is natural to feel anxious and overwhelmed. Remember, though, that you are not alone. God is with you every step of the way. His Word is full of promises of healing and restoration, and He is faithful to fulfil them.

Have faith, for Jesus said, "Everything is possible for one who believes" (Mark 9:23). Your belief is powerful, and your prayers are heard by the Almighty. When you pray for healing, you are not just speaking words into the air; you are calling upon the Creator of the universe, who loves you more than you can imagine.

God's Word reminds us, "The prayer of a righteous person is powerful and effective" (James 5:16). As you pray, trust that God is at work, even if you cannot see it immediately. He is the Great Physician, the Healer of all wounds, and the Restorer of broken hearts and bodies.

Believe in His promise: "By His wounds we are healed" (Isaiah 53:5). This means that Jesus has already borne your sickness and pain on the cross, and through His sacrifice, you have access to divine healing. Claim this promise with confidence and stand firm in your faith.

Miracles happen every day, and they can happen to you. Keep your heart open, your faith strong, and your prayers constant.

Trust in God's timing and His perfect plan for your life. Remember, "The Lord is close to the broken-hearted and saves those who are crushed in spirit" (Psalm 34:18). He sees your pain and is with you in every moment of your journey.

May you find peace in His presence, strength in His Word, and healing through His love. Keep believing, keep praying, and watch for the miracles that God will work in your life. He is with you, and He is faithful.

As you prepare to pray, remember to use the anointing oil as a symbol of your faith and dedication to God's promises. Anoint yourself, your home, and your loved ones, trusting in God's power to bring healing, protection, and favour.

With heartfelt encouragement.

Prayer for Healing

Most gracious and loving Father,

Today, I come before You with a heart full of gratitude for all You have done for me. Thank You, Lord, for this day You have given me, for the breath of life, and for Your beautiful creations. I praise You, Lord, and give You all the glory and honour. Thank You for loving me unconditionally.

Lord, Your Word speaks promises of healing and restoration, and today I stand on those promises. Your Word says, "I am the Lord who heals you" (Exodus 15:26). Strengthen me, Lord, during this time of illness. I have seen and heard of Your miracles before, and I know You can do it again. Father, I ask You to touch me now with that same power. I stand on Your unfailing promise that no weapon formed against me shall prosper (Isaiah 54:17). I thank You, Lord, that no sickness, no fear, or any oppression from the enemy will have power over my life.

Lord, Your Word says that the prayer of faith will heal the sick (James 5:15). Today, I come to You in faith asking for healing. Renew my mind, body, and soul. Your Word says, "Heal me, Lord, and I will be healed; save me and I will be saved, for You are the one I praise" (Jeremiah 17:14). Heal me, Lord, and make me whole again. Help me to focus on You and Your promises, not on my circumstances. Touch me, Lord, and restore my health.

Lord, give the doctors wisdom, knowledge, and understanding to treat me. In the midst of this trial, I put my faith and trust in You. I rebuke the spirit of fear and anything that is not of You. Your Word says, "By His wounds we are healed" (Isaiah 53:5). You took it all on the cross for me, Lord. Today, I claim this healing over my life. Touch me from the crown of my head to the soles of my feet. Breathe peace, healing, and calmness over me. Strengthen, guide, and protect me. Take Your rightful place, Lord, and speak life back into my body. Cover me with Your precious blood.

Father, You are Jehovah Rapha, the God who heals. You have done it before, Lord, do it again. Have Your way, Lord. Help me to feel Your presence and peace throughout today. I will continue to keep my eyes on You and trust that I will fully recover. I will hold tightly to Your promises. Thank You for being my Divine Healer.

I pray for victory over this sickness.

I ask all this in Jesus' precious name.

Amen.

Verse

James 5:15

> *And the prayer offered in faith will make the sick person well; the Lord will raise them up. If they have sinned, they will be forgiven."*

> ✯ ✯ ✯

> *Trust in God's healing power, for His love brings restoration and His strength carries us through every challenge.*

Daily Reflection

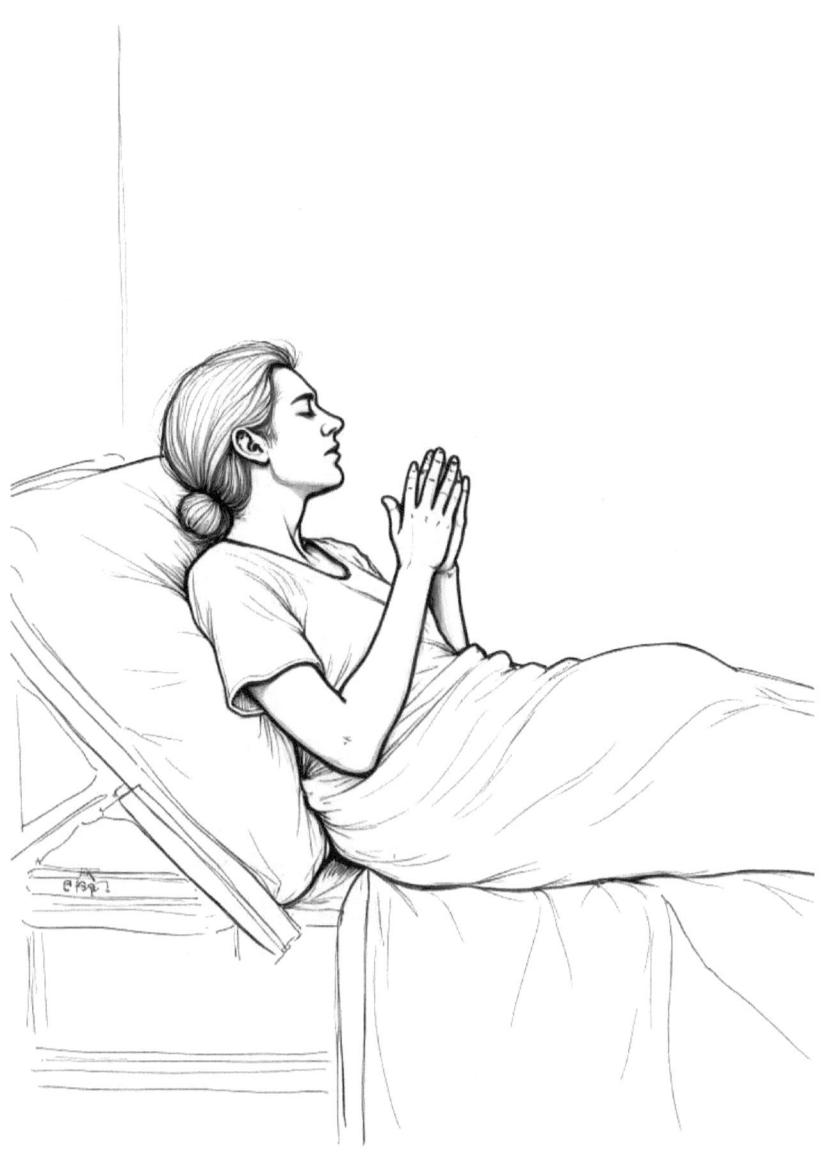

Prayer for Healing, Strength, and Divine Intervention in the Fight Against Cancer

Word of Encouragement

Dear Friend,

As you walk through this challenging journey, remember that you are not alone. The Lord is with you every step of the way, holding you in His loving arms. Your faith is a beacon of hope and strength, and it is through this faith that you will find the courage to face each day.

Take heart in knowing that God hears your prayers and sees your struggles. He is the Great Healer, and His promises are true. Trust in His timing and His plan for your life, knowing that He is working all things for your good.

Lean on Him for strength when you feel weak, and let His peace fill your heart when anxiety and fear threaten to overwhelm you. As Philippians 4:13 reminds us, "I can do all this through Him who gives me strength." Believe in the power of His love and the healing power of His blood.

Your faith is your greatest weapon against this illness. Hold onto it tightly, and let it be the foundation upon which you stand. Surround yourself with love, support, and positive affirmations, and know that countless prayers are being lifted on your behalf.

Every day is a step closer to your healing. Keep your eyes fixed on Jesus, the author and perfecter of our faith, and let His light guide you through the darkest times. You are stronger than you know, and with God by your side, you can overcome any obstacle.

Don't forget the power of anointing oil. As James 5:14-15 says, "Is anyone among you sick? Let them call the elders of the church to pray over them and anoint them with oil in the name of the Lord. And the prayer offered in faith will make the sick person well; the Lord will raise them up." Use the anointing oil as a symbol of God's presence and healing power, trusting in His promises.

May you find comfort in the arms of the Lord, and may His presence bring you peace, strength, and healing.

Please Note: *You can also use this prayer to intercede for someone else who is suffering from cancer. Simply insert their name and lift them up to the Lord, asking for His healing touch and divine intervention in their lives.*

With love and prayers.

Prayer for Healing, Strength, and Divine Intervention in the Fight Against Cancer

Our Dear Heavenly Father

I come before You today in the mighty name of Jesus, acknowledging Your boundless power and mercy. I plead the precious blood of Jesus over my body, mind, and spirit, believing in its power to heal, protect, and restore.

Lord Jesus, You endured suffering and death on the cross for our healing, as Your Word declares in Isaiah 53:5, "By His wounds we are healed." I claim this promise of healing through Your blood and ask that Your healing power flow through every part of my body, restoring it to perfect health.

Father, I declare victory over this illness through the blood of the Lamb, as Revelation 12:11 says, "They triumphed over him by the blood of the Lamb and by the word of their testimony." I stand firm in my faith, knowing Your blood has already conquered sin, sickness, and death. Strengthen my faith and help me testify of Your goodness and healing power.

Your Word assures us that "the blood of Jesus, His Son, purifies us from all sin" (1 John 1:7). Let Your blood purify me completely. I surrender my fears, doubts, and anxieties to You. Cover me with Your peace that surpasses all understanding, bringing physical, emotional, and spiritual renewal.

I pray in faith, trusting in Your promise that "the prayer offered in faith will make the sick person well" (James 5:15). I ask You to raise me up from this illness, granting me strength and vitality. Surround me with Your presence and let Your healing touch restore every part of me to wholeness.

Lord, I lift up to You the doctors, nurses, and all medical professionals involved in my care. As James 1:5 says, "If any of you lacks wisdom, you should ask God, who gives generously to all without finding fault." Grant them wisdom, knowledge, and discernment as they make decisions about my treatment. Guide their hands and minds and bless them with insight and compassion.

As I undergo treatments and prepare for surgery, grant me Your strength and peace. Philippians 4:13 reminds us, "I can do all this through Him who gives me strength." Help me endure each session, trusting in Your healing power. Let every treatment be effective and free from complications and side effects, and may Your presence be with me at every moment.

I choose to believe the report of the Lord, trusting in Your promises and power to heal. I reject any negative reports and focus on Your Word. Fill my heart with positivity and hope, knowing You are in control and desire good for me.

Help me to focus on You despite my discomfort and pain. As 2 Corinthians 12:9 says, "My grace is sufficient for you, for my power is made perfect in weakness." May my pain cease, my strength increase, and my fears be released as I prepare for surgery.

This disease has weakened my body, making rest difficult and energy scarce. I claim the promise of Matthew 11:28, "Come to me, all you who are weary and burdened, and I will give you rest." Please bless me with restful sleep and the energy I need to complete my tasks. Let Your healing touch bring me the rest and recovery my body so desperately needs.

Bless my body, Lord, and help me remain resilient and hopeful throughout this battle. I also lift up my family to You, asking that You grant them peace and comfort during this time. Surround us with Your love and support and give us the strength to face each day with courage.

Thank You, Jesus, for Your sacrifice and the power of Your blood. I trust in Your love and mercy. May Your will be done in

my life, and may Your name be glorified through my healing.
In the mighty name of Jesus, I pray.
Amen.

Verse

Jeremiah 17:14

> *"Heal me, Lord, and I will be healed; save me, and I will be saved, for you are the one I praise."*

✧ ✧ ✧

Remember, you are deeply loved and incredibly strong. Keep pressing forward, and never lose hope.

Daily Reflection

Prayer for Unemployment

Word of Encouragement

Dear Friend,

In the midst of your unemployment, it's natural to feel uncertain and anxious. But remember, this season is not the end of your story—it's a chapter in God's greater plan for your life. Hold on to the promise in Jeremiah 29:11: "For I know the plans I have for you, declares the Lord, plans to prosper you and not to harm you, plans to give you hope and a future." God's plans for you are filled with hope and a bright future, even when it seems difficult to see the way forward.

Believe that God is with you in this journey. He sees your struggles, hears your prayers, and knows your heart's desires. As Jesus reminds us in Matthew 7:7, "Ask, and it will be given to you; seek, and you will find; knock, and the door will be opened to you." Continue to ask, seek, and knock with faith, trusting that God will open the right door at the right time.

Faith as small as a mustard seed can move mountains (Matthew 17:20). Keep that faith alive in your heart. Trust that God is working behind the scenes, orchestrating opportunities and preparing you for the perfect job that aligns with your gifts and His purpose for you. He is Jehovah Jireh, your Provider, and He will not leave you or forsake you.

During this time, lean on His strength and wisdom. Let His Word be a source of comfort and encouragement. Remember Philippians 4:13, "I can do all things through Christ who strengthens me." You are not alone in this; God's strength will sustain you.

Stay positive, keep praying, and remain open to His guidance. Your breakthrough is coming. God is faithful, and He will provide. Trust in His timing and continue to believe in His goodness.

Pray this prayer with faith, believing in God's power to work miracles in your life. Use the anointing oil as a symbol of your faith and dedication to God's promises. May your faith be strengthened, and may you soon find the job that He has prepared for you. Keep your eyes on Him, and trust that He will lead you to a prosperous and fulfilling future.

With heartfelt encouragement.

Prayer for Unemployment

Our Dear Heavenly Father,

I call on You right now, trusting in Your promises and Your unfailing love. Your Word tells us that if we have faith as small as a mustard seed, we can move mountains (Matthew 17:20). Today, I put my faith and trust in You and ask that You open doors for me as I seek employment. Thank You for creating and moulding me with unique skills, abilities, gifts, and talents. Open my eyes to see the right opportunities where I can flourish and grow.

Lord, I sometimes struggle to understand how everything will work out, but today I place my trust in You. When I cannot see a way, I know that You will make a way (Isaiah 43:19). Help me to trust what is unseen. Thank You for the good things You have in store for those who love You and are called according to Your purpose (Romans 8:28).

Your Word says, "I can do all things through Christ who strengthens me" (Philippians 4:13). Increase my faith so that I may see Your favour in my life. I pray that the rest of this year will be filled with joy, peace, love, and hope. Please continue to watch over me and guide me. I pray for Your miracle-working power to bring favour and a breakthrough in my life. Awaken a new confidence in me, Lord, that I may receive all the blessings You have prepared for me.

Thank You for being my protector and provider. Your Word says that to those who ask, it shall be given; to those who seek, it will be found; and to those who knock, the door will be opened (Matthew 7:7). Help me to be a good steward over all that You have entrusted to me, as You make my way prosperous and successful (Joshua 1:8). Give me the peace of knowing that You will provide at all times.

Lord, I know that all things happen in Your perfect timing. My faith is in You, Lord, and I thank You in advance for what You are about to do. I know that every good and perfect gift comes from You (James 1:17). Your Word says, "For I know the plans I have for you, declares the Lord, plans to prosper you and not to harm you, plans to give you hope and a future" (Jeremiah 29:11). I claim this blessing in Jesus' name.

In Jesus' mighty name, I pray.

Amen.

Verse

Jeremiah 29:11

> *"For I know the plans I have for you, declares the Lord, plans to prosper you and not to harm you, plans to give you hope and a future."*

✦✦✦

When you pray with faith, God opens doors that lead to hope, prosperity, and a future filled with His blessings.

Daily Reflection

Prayer for Our Marriage

Word Encouragement

Dear Friend,

I want to encourage you as you pray for your marriage. Praying for your relationship is one of the most powerful things you can do, as it invites God's presence and guidance into every aspect of your life together.

Building your marriage on the foundation of God is essential for its strength and endurance. Your commitment to prayer demonstrates a deep desire to align your relationship with His will and to nurture it with His love and wisdom.

Psalm 147:3 beautifully assures us, "He heals the brokenhearted and binds up their wounds" (NIV). This promise reminds us that God is deeply invested in our well-being and is always ready to heal and restore. When you lift your marriage in prayer, you're asking for His healing touch and His ability to mend and strengthen your bond.

Jesus' words in Mark 10:9, "Therefore what God has joined together, let no one separate" (NIV), underscore the sacredness of marriage. By praying together and seeking God's guidance, you are honouring the divine covenant that He has established. This foundation not only supports your relationship but also invites His blessings and protection.

Using anointing oil as a symbol of your faith can enhance your prayers, serving as a tangible reminder of your trust in God's power to renew and fortify your marriage.

Remember, building a marriage on God's foundation involves more than just praying; it requires daily commitment, love, and mutual respect. As you seek God's guidance, He will provide the strength and wisdom needed to nurture a healthy, loving relationship. I believe that with God's support, your marriage will continue to grow and flourish.

With heartfelt prayers and encouragement.

Prayer for Our Marriage

Our Dear Heavenly Father,

Today, I come before You with a heart full of gratitude for the gift of marriage. Thank You for bringing us together and for Your plans to prosper us, as You declared in Your Word: "For I know the plans I have for you," declares the Lord, "plans to prosper you and not to harm you, plans to give you hope and a future" (Jeremiah 29:11, NIV). I pray that You bless and strengthen our marriage according to Your will.

Lord, be at the centre of our relationship. Remove any obstacles that stand in our way and draw us closer to You, as Your Word instructs: "Be completely humble and gentle; be patient, bearing with one another in love. Make every effort to keep the unity of the Spirit through the bond of peace" (Ephesians 4:2-3, NIV). Teach us to forgive one another just as You have forgiven us, following the wisdom of: "Bear with each other and forgive one another if any of you has a grievance against someone. Forgive as the Lord forgave you" (Colossians 3:13, NIV). Help us to communicate with love and kindness, remembering that "A gentle answer turns away wrath, but a harsh word stirs up anger" (Proverbs 15:1, NIV).

Grant me the selflessness to prioritise my spouse's needs above my own, as You said: "Do nothing out of selfish ambition or vain conceit. Rather, in humility value others above yourselves, not looking to your own interests but each of you to the interests of the others" (Philippians 2:3-4, NIV). Strengthen our commitment to each other and help us seek forgiveness when we falter.

Guide us in making decisions together, especially concerning our finances, as Your Word highlights: "Plans fail for lack of counsel, but with many advisers they succeed" (Proverbs 15:22,

NIV). Bless us abundantly so that we may bless others, in line with: "And God is able to bless you abundantly, so that in all things at all times, having all that you need, you will abound in every good work" (2 Corinthians 9:8, NIV).

May our love reflect Your love for the church, filled with unity, respect, and understanding, as You instructed: "Husbands, love your wives, just as Christ loved the church and gave himself up for her" (Ephesians 5:25, NIV). Let our marriage be a testament to Your glory and help us build each other up and grow stronger in our union daily. As Your Word assures us: "It always protects, always trusts, always hopes, always perseveres. Love never fails" (1 Corinthians 13:7-8, NIV).

For those who are struggling, Lord, I ask for Your healing touch. Heal our hearts and our relationship and fill our home with Your peace and joy. Help us to remember that a marriage built on Your foundation can withstand any storm. Grant us strength to face challenges together, trusting in Your promise: "With man this is impossible, but with God all things are possible" (Matthew 19:26, NIV). Even when we face darkness and things don't go as planned, help us to see Your light. Strengthen our faith in each other and in You, Lord, and help us to focus on You and lean closer to You, remembering: "Be strong and courageous. Do not be afraid or terrified because of them, for the Lord your God goes with you; he will never leave you nor forsake you" (Deuteronomy 31:6, NIV).

May our love be a reflection of Your grace and mercy, bringing glory to Your name. We trust that You are always with us, guiding us through every situation.

In Jesus' precious name, I pray,
Amen.

Verse

Mark 10:9 (NIV)

"Therefore, what God has joined together, let no one separate."

✭✭✭

God's love and prayer can heal and strengthen marriages, restoring them with enduring love and unity.

Daily Reflection

Prayer for All Men in our Lives

Word of Encouragement

Dear Friend,

As you lift up the men in your life in prayer, know that your prayers are powerful and effective. The Bible assures us that when we pray according to God's will, He hears us (1 John 5:14). Your heartfelt intercession for your fathers, grandfathers, husbands, sons, and all the significant men in your life is a testament to your faith and love for them.

God delights in our prayers for others, and He promises to bless those who seek Him on behalf of others. Your prayers are not in vain; they are a source of strength, guidance, and protection for those you pray for. Trust in God's timing and His perfect plan for each of them.

Continue to pray with faith, believing that God is at work in their lives, even when you may not see immediate results. Your perseverance in prayer makes a difference and aligns with God's heart for His people. May you be encouraged by His faithfulness and the assurance that He hears every word spoken in faith.

Keep lifting them up in prayer, knowing that your love and dedication to seeking God's best for them is deeply impactful. May God continue to use your prayers to bring about His purposes and blessings in their lives.

With heartfelt encouragement.

Prayer for All Men in our Lives

The Bible teaches us that the prayer of a righteous person is powerful and effective. Today, we lift up in prayer the MEN in our lives—our fathers, grandfathers, husbands, sons, brothers, nephews, cousins, uncles, partners, fiancés, boyfriends, friends, and all who impact our lives. Prayer is powerful; let us pray this prayer over them with faith.

Our Dear Heavenly Father,

Thank You for Your Word, which guides our steps and illuminates our path in life. Today, I come before You on behalf of Your sons, seeking Your divine favour and blessing upon them. May they walk in ways that are pleasing to You, looking to You as their ultimate source of strength and guidance, as Psalm 32:8 assures us that You will instruct and teach us in the way we should go.

Father, I pray that You overflow their lives with Your abundant blessings. In moments of weariness and pressure from the world, may they find rest and renewal in Your presence, just as Matthew 11:28 promises that You will give rest to all who are weary and burdened. Grant them the wisdom and discernment to make choices that align with Your will, leading them on paths of righteousness, as Proverbs 3:5-6 instructs us to trust in You with all our hearts and acknowledge You in all our ways.

Lord, guard their hearts and minds with Your peace that surpasses all understanding, as Philippians 4:7 reminds us that Your peace will guard our hearts and minds in Christ Jesus. When fear or turmoil grips their hearts, empower them with Your spirit of courage, love, and a sound mind, as 2 Timothy 1:7 assures us that You have given us a spirit not of fear but of power, love, and self-discipline. Protect them from every temptation and lead them away from paths that would lead them astray, knowing that 1 Corinthians 10:13 promises that You will provide a way out so that we can endure it.

Father, fill their lives with Your love, joy, and faithfulness. May they be beacons of light in their communities, shining Your truth and grace wherever they go, as Matthew 5:16 encourages us to let our light shine before others, that they may see our good deeds and glorify our Father in heaven. Strengthen them to overcome every challenge and obstacle they face, knowing that in You, they are more than conquerors, as Romans 8:37 declares.

Establish the work of their hands, Lord. Help them to be diligent, productive, patient, and wise in their endeavours, as Proverbs 16:3 teaches us to commit to the Lord whatever we do, and our plans will succeed. Keep them focused on Your purposes, guarding them against distractions that would hinder their service to You, remembering Colossians 3:23-24, which instructs us to work heartily as for the Lord and not for men, knowing that we will receive an inheritance from the Lord as a reward. Teach them to prioritise their relationships—with You, their families, and their communities—so that their lives may bring glory to Your name, as Matthew 22:37-39 commands us to love You with all our heart, soul, and mind, and to love our neighbours as ourselves.

We lift all these prayers in the mighty name of Jesus, believing in Your power to transform lives and circumstances.

In Jesus' precious name, I pray,

Amen.

Verse

1 Timothy 2:1 (NIV)

"I urge, then, first of all, that petitions, prayers, intercession and thanksgiving be made for all people."

✧✧✧

Prayer has the power to uplift and transform the lives of the men we hold dear, bringing God's blessings and strength into their journey.

Daily Reflection

Prayer for All Women in our Lives

Word of Encouragement

Dear Sisters in Christ,

As we lift each other up in prayer, remember that our prayers are powerful and effective When we intercede for one another with genuine love and faith, we align ourselves with God's heart for His daughters. Let us encourage each other to keep pressing forward in faith, knowing that God hears our prayers and delights in answering them according to His will.

May our prayers for each other be a source of strength, comfort, and encouragement. Let us pray for wisdom, guidance, and protection over one another (James 1:5; Psalm 91:11), believing that God is faithful to fulfil His promises. As we support each other in prayer, may we grow in unity, love, and faith, reflecting the beauty of Christ in our relationships (Colossians 3:14).

Sisters, continue to lift each other up in prayer, knowing that God is at work in and through our lives. Let us walk together in faith, trusting that God's plans for each of us are good and filled with hope. May our prayers strengthen our bond as sisters in Christ and bring glory to His name.

In His love.

Prayer for all Woman in our lives

Dear Heavenly Father,

We come before You today with hearts full of gratitude for the women You have placed in our lives—wives, daughters, sisters, nieces, grandmothers, aunts, friends, and all who bless us with their love and presence

Your Word teaches us that a woman of noble character is worth more than rubies (Proverbs 31:10), and we thank You for each one who embodies Your wisdom and grace.

Father, we lift up all women to You. Thank You for their love, strength, and resilience. May they continue to walk in Your ways, finding their identity and worth in You alone (Proverbs 3:15-18). Grant them wisdom and discernment in every decision they make and fill their hearts with Your peace that surpasses all understanding (Philippians 4:6-7).

We pray for women of all ages. Protect them and guide them as they grow. Instil in them a deep love for You and a desire to follow Your path for their lives (Psalm 119:105). May they be women of integrity and grace, shining Your light wherever they go (Matthew 5:16).

Bless women with Your favour and provision. Strengthen their faith and grant them the desires of their hearts as they delight in You (Psalm 37:4). May they find joy and fulfilment in Your presence and draw near to You daily (James 4:8).

We ask for Your grace and mercy for women in all roles and stages of life. Surround them with Your love and protection. May they be examples of faith and courage, inspiring those around them with Your love (Psalm 31:24).

Lord, we lift up our friends who bless our lives with their companionship and support. May they experience Your peace and joy in abundance. Give them strength in times of trial and comfort in times of sorrow (Isaiah 41:10).

Father, You are the giver of every good and perfect gift (James 1:17), and we thank You for the precious women in our lives. Help us to cherish and honour them as You do. May our relationships reflect Your love and grace, bringing glory to Your name.

In Jesus' precious name, I pray,
Amen.

Verse

Proverbs 31:30 (NIV)

"Charm is deceptive, and beauty is fleeting; but a woman who fears the Lord is to be praised."

✯✯✯

Prayer connects our hearts as sisters in Christ, empowering us to uplift, strengthen, and honour each other in God's love.

Daily Reflection

Prayer Over Debt and Finances

Word of Encouragement

Dear Friend,

As you pray for financial blessing and provision, remember that God hears your prayers and cares deeply for your needs. The Bible assures us in Philippians 4:19 that God will supply all our needs according to His riches in glory through Christ Jesus. This promise is not just a hope but a firm assurance that God is faithful to His word.

Believe in the power of prayer and trust in God's provision. Use the anointing oil as a symbol of your faith and dependence on God's guidance and favour in your financial matters. Remember, God is Jehovah Jireh, your provider, and He delights in blessing His children abundantly.

Stay steadfast in faith, knowing that God's timing and ways are perfect. Keep praying, keep believing, and watch as God moves in your life to meet every need and exceed every expectation.

May you experience the joy of God's provision and the peace that comes from trusting in His unfailing promises.

In His love.

Prayer Over Debt and Finances

Our Dear Heavenly Father,

Your word assures me not to be anxious about anything, but in every situation, through prayer and petition, with thanksgiving, to present my requests to You (Philippians 4:6). Today, I come before You in the mighty name of Jesus, laying my finances at Your feet. I pray for a financial blessing in my life, Lord, knowing that You are my provider, Jehovah Jireh (Genesis 22:14).

Father, Your promise is that You will supply all my needs according to Your riches in glory in Christ Jesus (Philippians 4:19). Grant me wisdom to be a faithful steward of the resources You have entrusted to me (Luke 16:10-11). I ask for debt cancellation and a breakthrough in my financial situation. Help me to manage my finances wisely and to honour You with my wealth (Proverbs 3:9-10).

Lord, nothing is impossible with You (Luke 1:37). I pray for a financial breakthrough and prosperity in my life. Enlarge my territory so that I can be a blessing to others as You have blessed me (1 Chronicles 4:10). Close doors that no one can shut and open doors that no one can close, according to Your divine will and purpose (Revelation 3:7).

I declare victory and prosperity not only in my life but also in my family's life. I bind every spirit of hindrance and destruction that seeks to block Your blessings in my life. I break every financial stronghold and mindset of poverty. Renew my mind, O Lord, so that I may trust fully in You and Your provision (Romans 12:2).

Lord, bless my coming in and my going out (Deuteronomy 28:6). Let Your blessings chase me down and overtake me (Deuteronomy 28:2). May Your favour rest upon me and may I

experience Your abundance in every area of my life.
   In Jesus' mighty name,
   Amen.

Verse

Philippians 4:19 (NIV)

"And my God will meet all your needs according to the riches of his glory in Christ Jesus."

✯✯✯

Pray faithfully, trust in God's provision, and watch as He turns financial challenges into testimonies of His abundant blessings.

Daily Reflection

Prayer Over my Business

Word Encouragement

Dear Friend,

As you lift up your business in prayer, remember that God is attentive to your every need and aspiration. Your commitment to seek His guidance and favour is a testament to your faith and reliance on His promises. Trust that He sees your efforts, hears your prayers, and is already at work in ways that surpass your understanding.

The Bible assures us in Philippians 4:6-7, "Do not be anxious about anything, but in everything by prayer and supplication with thanksgiving let your requests be made known to God. And the peace of God, which surpasses all understanding, will guard your hearts and your minds in Christ Jesus." Hold fast to this promise as you navigate the challenges and opportunities in your business journey.

Continue to align your plans with His will, knowing that He directs the steps of those who acknowledge Him (Proverbs 3:5-6). Stay encouraged, knowing that God's timing and provision are perfect. May His grace and wisdom guide you in every decision, and may His favour rest upon your business, bringing forth prosperity and blessing to you and others.

Trust in His unfailing love and His promise to provide for all your needs. Keep praying, keep believing, and keep pressing forward in faith.

In His strength and peace.

Prayer Over my Business

Our Dear Heavenly Father,

Today, I humbly come before You in the precious name of Jesus, grateful for the opportunity to bring my business before You in prayer. Your word instructs us to pray without ceasing and to give thanks in everything, for this is Your will for us (1 Thessalonians 5:16-18). Lord, I thank You for the vision and plan You have given me for my business, knowing that every good and perfect gift comes from You (James 1:17).

Father, I ask for Your power, grace, and mercy to be upon my business. You have entrusted me with this responsibility, and I seek Your wisdom and guidance in all that I do (Proverbs 3:5-6). Remove all financial hindrances that stand in the way of the success and prosperity You have ordained for my business. Open my mind and heart to recognise new opportunities and avenues for growth (Isaiah 43:19).

I declare by faith that I trust in Your ability to bring about a turnaround in my business. Your word reminds me that You care for the birds of the air and how much more valuable I am to You (Matthew 6:26). I claim Your promises of provision and blessing over my business today.

Lord, I acknowledge that I cannot succeed alone. I ask for Your favour to rest upon me and Your divine guidance to lead me forward (Psalm 5:12). In these challenging times, I trust in Your promise to make a way where there seems to be no way (Isaiah 43:16).

I break and bind every cycle of failure and declare that my business is established upon Your principles of success and prosperity. Help me to make wise choices, to operate with fairness and honesty in all my dealings (Proverbs 11:3). Grant me integrity in every interaction with my staff, customers, and suppliers, reflecting Your love and respect in all I do.

Father, I ask You to reveal new opportunities and open doors for expansion according to Your will (Revelation 3:8). Bless my business abundantly so that it may be a source of blessing to others as well (Psalm 115:14).

Thank You, Lord, for Your promise to supply all my needs according to Your riches in glory through Christ Jesus (Philippians 4:19). I receive Your release of prosperity over my business today and commit my journey into Your hands, trusting in Your generous provision and unfailing guidance.

In Jesus' mighty name,
Amen.

Verse

Proverbs 16:3

> *"Commit your work to the Lord, and your plans will be established."*

✹✹✹

Commit your business endeavours to God's guidance and watch His plans unfold in ways that exceed your expectations.

Daily Reflection

Prayer for Anxiety and Depression

Word Encouragement

Dear Friend,

As you pray this heartfelt prayer, know that you are not alone in your struggles. The Lord is with you, ready to bring comfort and peace to your heart. Have faith and believe that He hears you and will respond to your cries.

"Do not be anxious about anything, but in every situation, by prayer and petition, with thanksgiving, present your requests to God. And the peace of God, which transcends all understanding, will guard your hearts and your minds in Christ Jesus" (Philippians 4:6-7).

Hold on to this promise, and trust that God's peace, which is beyond human understanding, will fill your heart and mind. Take a step of faith and anoint yourself with anointing oil as a symbol of God's presence and healing power in your life. As you do, remember that the anointing oil represents the Holy Spirit's work in you, bringing comfort, strength, and renewal.

Keep praying, keep believing, and keep trusting in God's unwavering love and faithfulness. He is your refuge and strength, your ever-present help in times of trouble. May His peace reign in your heart and His joy be your strength.

In faith and hope.

Prayer for Anxiety and Depression

Dear Heavenly Father,

I come before You today with a heavy heart, burdened by anxiety and weighed down by the darkness of depression. Your Word reminds me that You are near to the broken-hearted and save the crushed in spirit (Psalm 34:18). Lord, I cling to Your promise that You will never leave me nor forsake me (Deuteronomy 31:6).

Father, in the midst of my struggles, I find comfort in knowing that You are my refuge and strength, a very present help in trouble (Psalm 46:1). When my soul is weary and restless, I pray for Your peace that surpasses all understanding to guard my heart and mind in Christ Jesus (Philippians 4:7).

Lord Jesus, You understand every pain and sorrow. You bore our griefs and carried our sorrows on the cross (Isaiah 53:4). I lift up my burdens to You and ask for Your healing touch upon my mind and emotions. Fill me with Your love, for perfect love casts out fear (1 John 4:18).

Holy Spirit, You are my Comforter and Counsellor. Guide me through this season, renewing my strength like the eagles (Isaiah 40:31). Help me to trust in You with all my heart and lean not on my own understanding, but in all my ways acknowledge You, knowing that You will direct my paths (Proverbs 3:5-6).

Thank You, Lord, for Your faithfulness and Your promise to give me hope and a future (Jeremiah 29:11). May Your peace reign in my heart and Your joy be my strength.

Lord, we thank You for Your mighty hand in our lives. You are in control, and You work every detail for our good and for Your glory (Romans 8:28). Even amid the unknown, which may cause anxiety and depression, we choose to trust You and rest in Your sovereignty. We surrender everything to You, even our silent battles. Remove our burdens, worries, fears, doubts, and troubles. Release us from the pain of past hurts, the present anger, and the tension of future fears. Renew us, give us new strength, hope, and confidence to meet the constant struggles of daily life with a deeper faith and trust in You (Isaiah 40:31).

We are so thankful that You guide, protect, and hold us together (Psalm 32:8). Today we ask for complete peace and comfort. Continue to strengthen our faith in You. Lord, let Your love set us free (Galatians 5:1). Help us to be a light to others who also need You (Matthew 5:14-16).

In Jesus' precious name, I pray,

Amen.

Verse

Philippians 4:6-7 (NIV)

> *"Do not be anxious about anything, but in every situation, by prayer and petition, with thanksgiving, present your requests to God. And the peace of God, which transcends all understanding, will guard your hearts and your minds in Christ Jesus."*
>
> ✰✰✰
>
> *In the midst of anxiety and depression, find peace in God's presence, strength in His promises, and hope in His unfailing love.*

Daily Reflection

Prayer for Thanks and Gratitude

Word of Encouragement

Dear Friend,

As you pour out your heart in gratitude to our Heavenly Father, may you feel His presence surrounding you with peace and joy. Remember that your thankfulness opens the door to His blessings and shifts your focus from challenges to His unwavering love and provision.

"Give thanks to the Lord, for He is good; His love endures forever" (Psalm 107:1). Let this truth anchor your soul and remind you that God is always with you, guiding and supporting you through every step of your journey. Embrace each day with a grateful heart, knowing that His grace and mercy are renewed every morning. Your gratitude is a powerful testament to His goodness, and it will illuminate your path with hope and strength.

Be encouraged, for you are cherished and deeply loved by the One who holds all things together. Continue to trust in Him and watch as He works all things for your good.

With heartfelt blessings and love.

Prayer for Thanks and Gratitude

Our Dear Heavenly Father,

I come before You with a heart full of gratitude and thankfulness. Your Word says, "Give thanks to the Lord, for He is good; His love endures forever" (Psalm 107:1). Today, I thank You for Your unending love and faithfulness.

Lord, I am grateful for every blessing You have bestowed upon me. Your Word reminds me, "Every good and perfect gift is from above, coming down from the Father of the heavenly lights, who does not change like shifting shadows" (James 1:17). Thank You for Your steadfast provision and for showering my life with good things.

Thank You, Father, for the gift of life and the breath in my lungs. As it says in Your Word, "I will give thanks to You, Lord, with all my heart; I will tell of all Your wonderful deeds" (Psalm 9:1). I am grateful for the beauty of Your creation, for the joy of family and friends, and for the opportunities to experience Your love in countless ways.

Lord, I am especially thankful for Your presence in my life. "The Lord is my strength and my shield; my heart trusts in Him, and He helps me. My heart leaps for joy, and with my song I praise Him" (Psalm 28:7). Your guidance, protection, and constant companionship bring me great comfort and joy.

Thank You for Your grace and mercy, renewed each day. "Because of the Lord's great love, we are not consumed, for His compassions never fail. They are new every morning; great is Your faithfulness" (Lamentations 3:22-23). I am humbled by Your forgiveness and the new beginnings You offer me.

As I reflect on Your goodness, I pray that my life may be a testament to Your love and grace. Help me to have a grateful heart in all circumstances, as Your Word teaches, "Give thanks in all circumstances; for this is God's will for you in Christ Jesus" (1 Thessalonians 5:18).

Father, in Psalms 100:4-5, Your Word says, "Enter his gates with thanksgiving, and his courts with praise! Give thanks to him; bless his name! For the Lord is good; his steadfast love endures forever, and his faithfulness to all generations." Today, Father, I am reminded that You are the giver of all good gifts. Thank You, Lord, that every good and perfect gift comes from You. Thank You, Father, for the very breath of life, for the ability to love and be loved, for all Your beautiful creations, and for all that You have blessed me with.

Lord, I know that You are with me every step of the way, even when things seem challenging, unfair, or difficult. I know that the best way to defeat the enemy's attack on me is through a grateful heart. Your ways are far greater than our ways, and Your thoughts are far deeper than our thoughts. Today, I thank You for Your daily, powerful presence in our lives. Your Word says that even though I walk through the darkest valley, I will fear no evil, for You are with me; Your rod and Your staff, they comfort me. Thank You, Lord, for Your strength and protection, for Your blood covering over me.

Thank You that neither death nor life, angels nor rulers, things present nor future, height nor depth, nor anything else in all creation, will be able to separate me from Your love. I am so grateful and thankful to You. You are good and faithful, and Your love endures forever. I know that nothing is impossible for You. Thank You for Your compassion and mercy to Your children. Thank You that You know my every need, and I have seen Your mighty hand move in my life. Thank You for forgiving our sins, taking away our suffering, pain, and tears, and healing our diseases. Thank You for conquering the powers of Satan, sin, and death.

Thank You, Lord, for all that You have done for me and all

that You are going to do. I rest in You, believing You're working all things for good in my life. Come and have Your way in me. Help me to lean closer to You. I come before You with a grateful and thankful heart.

I ask all this through Jesus Christ, our Lord.

Amen.

Verse

Psalm 107:1

"Give thanks to the Lord, for He is good; His love endures forever."

✯ ✯ ✯

Gratitude turns what we have into enough, and more. It is the key that unlocks God's blessings in our lives.

Daily Reflection

Powerful Prayer to Break Generational Curses

Word of Encouragement

Dear Beloved,

As you come before the Lord in prayer, know that your Heavenly Father hears every word and sees every tear. Trust in His promises and believe in His power to break every chain and set you free from any generational curse that may be affecting your family. God's Word is true and His love for you is everlasting.

Pray with unwavering faith, knowing that "if you have faith as small as a mustard seed, you can say to this mountain, 'Move from here to there,' and it will move. Nothing will be impossible for you" (Matthew 17:20). Stand firm in the authority given to you by Jesus Christ, who said, "Behold, I give you the authority to trample on serpents and scorpions, and over all the power of the enemy, and nothing shall by any means hurt you" (Luke 10:19).

As you pray, I encourage you to use anointing oil to anoint yourself, your family, and your home. Anointing with oil is a powerful symbol of God's presence and blessing. It is an act of faith that signifies your trust in God's protection and deliverance. Remember, "Is anyone among you sick? Let them call the elders of the church to pray over them and anoint them with oil in the name of the Lord" (James 5:14).

Believe that God is working mightily in your life and in the lives of your loved ones. Declare His victory over every curse and walk in the freedom and blessings that Jesus has secured for you. You are a new creation in Christ, and His love, peace, and righteousness will flow through you and your family for generations to come.

Be encouraged, be strong, and know that God is with you every step of the way.

In Christ's love and grace.

Powerful Prayer to Break Generational Curses

Our Dear Heavenly Father,

I come before You today, acknowledging Your power and sovereignty over my life. I stand on the promises in Your Word and seek Your deliverance from any generational curses that may be affecting my family and me. Your Word declares, "Christ redeemed us from the curse of the law by becoming a curse for us" (Galatians 3:13). I claim that redemption and declare freedom in the name of Jesus.

Lord, Your Word also says, "The Lord is slow to anger, abounding in love and forgiving sin and rebellion. Yet He does not leave the guilty unpunished; He punishes the children for the sin of the parents to the third and fourth generation" (Numbers 14:18). I acknowledge any sins and iniquities of my ancestors that may have brought curses upon my family line. I repent and renounce those sins, asking for Your forgiveness and cleansing. I thank You, Father, for the assurance that "if we confess our sins, He is faithful and just and will forgive us our sins and purify us from all unrighteousness" (1 John 1:9). I confess and renounce any known and unknown sins that have opened the door to curses in my family. I ask for Your purification and cleansing from all unrighteousness.

Your Word promises, "If anyone is in Christ, the new creation has come: The old has gone, the new is here!" (2 Corinthians 5:17). I declare that I am a new creation in Christ, and the old generational curses have no power over me. I break every chain of bondage and declare that they are null and void in Jesus' name. Father, I stand on Your promise in Ezekiel 18:20: "The one who sins is the one who will die. The child will not share the guilt of the parent, nor will the parent share the guilt of the child." I declare that I am no longer bound by the sins of my ancestors. I am set free by the blood of Jesus, and I walk in the liberty that Christ has given me.

I also claim the promise in Isaiah 54:17, "No weapon forged against you will prevail, and you will refute every tongue that accuses you. This is the heritage of the servants of the Lord, and this is their vindication from me," declares the Lord. I declare that no generational curse, no weapon formed against me, will prevail. I stand in the victory of Christ and refute any accusation against me by the enemy.

Lord, I pray for Your healing and restoration in my family. I ask that You break every cycle of sin, addiction, and destructive behaviour. Restore what the enemy has stolen and bring Your peace and wholeness to my family. Your Word says, "But from everlasting to everlasting the Lord's love is with those who fear Him, and His righteousness with their children's children" (Psalm 103:17). I claim this promise for my family, and I trust in Your everlasting love and righteousness.

We thank You, Lord, that we are a new creation in Christ. We refuse to be bound by chains of generational curses. Lord, I pray that they will have no power over me or my family. I pray that every curse spoken, written, or transferred to me is broken by the blood of Jesus. I pray against poverty, sickness, divorce, barrenness, anger, alcoholism, drugs, premature death, shame, debt, dysfunctional lifestyles, lying, bitterness, gossiping, oaths, rituals, vows, and anything else that is not of You, because who the Son has set free is free indeed. We pray, Lord, that they will never manifest in our lives. We bind every curse or any negativity that has passed on in our family from generation to generation. Father, we pray that You remove anything that is not of You. I break the power of the enemy over our lives. We declare that every curse that the enemy has against us is null and void. We reject every curse in our family line and choose to walk in Your love and blessings. We plead the blood of Jesus Christ over our family and declare that these curses will not have any hold over us or future generations to come.

We now claim every spiritual blessing You have given to us in Christ Jesus (Ephesians 1:3). We know that Satan comes to steal, kill, and destroy, and we know that You came that we may have life and have it abundantly. We thank You, Lord, for dying on the cross for us; because of Your great sacrifice, we know that my family and I have been set free from generational curses. Help us, Lord, as we seek Your face in breaking the chains that have held us captive and in bondage. By the blood of Jesus Christ, I break the power and hold of every curse that has come to our family. Thank You, Lord, that my family and I are now free from any and all generational curses in Jesus' Name!

In Jesus' precious name, I pray,

Amen.

Verse

Luke 10:19

> *"Behold, I give you the authority to trample on serpents and scorpions, and over all the power of the enemy, and nothing shall by any means hurt you."*

✩✩✩

> *By the authority of Jesus Christ, generational curses are nullified, chains of bondage are broken, and we walk in the freedom and blessings of God's love.*

Daily Reflection

Prayer for Peace

Word of Encouragement

Dear Friend,

May you find comfort in knowing that God's peace, which surpasses all understanding, is available to you. In the midst of life's chaos and uncertainties, may His calming presence fill your heart and mind. Remember His promise: "Peace I leave with you; my peace I give you. I do not give to you as the world gives. Do not let your hearts be troubled and do not be afraid" (John 14:27). Trust in His faithfulness to guard and guide you through every situation. May you experience His peace that transcends all circumstances, bringing you strength, hope, and assurance. Keep leaning on Him, and He will sustain you with His perfect peace.

Blessings to you.

Prayer for Peace

I come before You today, seeking Your peace that surpasses all understanding. In this chaotic world, I long for the calm assurance that only You can provide. Your Word assures me, "Peace I leave with you; my peace I give you. I do not give to you as the world gives. Do not let your hearts be troubled and do not be afraid" (John 14:27). Lord, I hold fast to this promise, asking that Your peace fill my heart and mind.

Father, I lift up to You my anxieties, fears, and worries. Your Word encourages me, "Do not be anxious about anything, but in every situation, by prayer and petition, with thanksgiving, present your requests to God. And the peace of God, which transcends all understanding, will guard your hearts and your minds in Christ Jesus" (Philippians 4:6-7). Grant me Your peace that surpasses all understanding, guarding my heart and mind.

Lord, I pray for peace in my relationships. Help me to embody the spirit of a peacemaker, as You have called me to be: "Blessed are the peacemakers, for they will be called children of God" (Matthew 5:9). Grant me wisdom to navigate conflicts with grace and love, and to seek reconciliation wherever possible. Let Your love and peace flow through me to those around me.

I ask for Your peace to dwell in my home, making it a sanctuary filled with Your presence and love. Your promise comforts me: "My people will live in peaceful dwelling places, in secure homes, in undisturbed places of rest" (Isaiah 32:18). May my home be a place of rest and refuge, free from strife and discord.

Today, I surrender all my burdens—worries, fears, anxieties—to You. Your Word reassures me: "Do not be anxious about anything. Instead, in every situation, by prayer and petition, with thanksgiving, present your requests to God. And the peace of God, which transcends all understanding, will guard your hearts and your minds in Christ Jesus" (Philippians 4:6-7). I claim Your promises of peace, strength, and protection over my life. Grant me a peace that goes beyond human understanding, and let Your angels protect and comfort me.

Father, help me to fix my mind, heart, and soul on You, knowing that perfect peace, love, and joy come from You alone. Even amidst uncertainties, temptations, and challenges, I trust in Your presence with me. Help me to focus my thoughts on what is true, honourable, right, pure, lovely, and admirable. Teach me to dwell on these things.

Lord, I stand firm on Your Word, claiming Your perfect peace that drives out fear and frees me from worldly concerns. You are my refuge and fortress; in You, I place my trust. Thank You, Lord, that no harm can overcome me and that I find safety in You alone. I leave all my requests, worries, cares, and concerns in Your hands, knowing that my safe place is with You. Give me the courage and confidence to face each day, keeping my eyes fixed on You.

Father, Your Word commands me to be strong and courageous, not to be afraid or discouraged, for You are with me wherever I go. Fill my soul with peace that surpasses worldly understanding, making me a beacon of Your love to others. I commit my family to Your care; bring them peace and protection, and lead us away from hate and anger, guiding us into love, joy, and abundant peace.

Help me, Lord, to trust fully in Your control over all things, finding perfect peace in You alone. In Your perfect love, I ask for these blessings and promises to be fulfilled in my life.

In Jesus' precious name, I pray,
Amen.

Verse

John 14:27

"Peace, I leave with you; my peace I give you. I do not give to you as the world gives. Do not let your hearts be troubled and do not be afraid."

✯✯✯

In the presence of God's peace, fears fade, burdens lift, and hope rises, for His peace surpasses all understanding.

Daily Reflection

Prayer for a Peaceful Sleep

Word of Encouragement

Dear Friend,

As you seek peace and rest tonight, I want to encourage you with these words. Remember that God's love and peace are always with you, especially in the quiet moments of the night.

Tonight, as you lay down, may you find solace in His presence. Trust in His promises to guard your heart and mind and know that He cares deeply for you. Rest peacefully, knowing that His love surrounds you and His angels watch over you through the night.

Take comfort in His unfailing grace and mercy. Allow His peace to settle your soul and bring you the rest you need. May you wake up refreshed, renewed, and ready to face each new day knowing that you are deeply loved and cherished by Him.

With prayers for a peaceful night.

Prayer for a Peaceful Sleep

Our Dear Heavenly Father,

As I prepare to rest, I come before You, grateful for the day You have provided. Your Word assures me, "In peace, I will lie down and sleep, for you alone, Lord, make me dwell in safety" (Psalm 4:8). Father, I seek Your peace that surpasses all understanding to guard my heart and mind as I sleep.

Lord, I cast all my anxieties and concerns upon You, knowing that You care for me (1 Peter 5:7). Please calm my thoughts and grant me a tranquil heart. Your Word promises, "You will keep in perfect peace those whose minds are steadfast, because they trust in you" (Isaiah 26:3). Help me to trust You completely tonight.

I pray for protection throughout the night. Your angels are encamped around those who fear You, guarding them day and night (Psalm 34:7). I ask for Your angels to surround my home and keep me safe from all harm and evil.

Father, forgive me for any sins I have committed today. Wash me clean with Your grace and mercy. Your Word assures me, "If we confess our sins, he is faithful and just and will forgive us our sins and purify us from all unrighteousness" (1 John 1:9).

As I lie down to sleep, I entrust my loved ones and all that concerns me into Your loving hands. May Your peace reign in my home, and may I awaken refreshed and renewed to serve You.

Lord, I know Your Word is alive and powerful, calming my anxious heart and restless mind. Tonight, I cast all my worries and cares upon You, trusting for a full night's rest. Bless me now with peaceful sleep. Let Your angels take charge over me, covering me with Your protective hand.

Thank You, Lord, for Your unfailing love, mercy, and grace.

Grant me a restorative night's sleep so that I can awaken refreshed and ready to serve You anew. Help me fix my eyes and heart on You, knowing You hold everything together.

Your Word says, "Do not be anxious about anything, but in every situation, by prayer and petition, with thanksgiving, present your requests to God. And the peace of God, which transcends all understanding, will guard your hearts and your minds in Christ Jesus" (Philippians 4:6-7). I claim this peace in my life today. Quiet and calm my mind, Lord, and guard my heart against fear and worry, which are not from You.

Renew my body, mind, and spirit tonight, Lord, that I may experience the peace You desire for me. As I lay my burdens at Your feet, grant me the blessing of rest and peaceful sleep.

In the mighty name of Jesus,
Amen.

Verse

2 Thessalonians 3:16

"May the Lord of peace Himself give you peace at all times and in every way. The Lord be with all of you."

✷✷✷

In the quiet of the night, may God's peace blanket your soul, guiding you into restful sleep and awakening you with renewed strength.

Daily Reflection

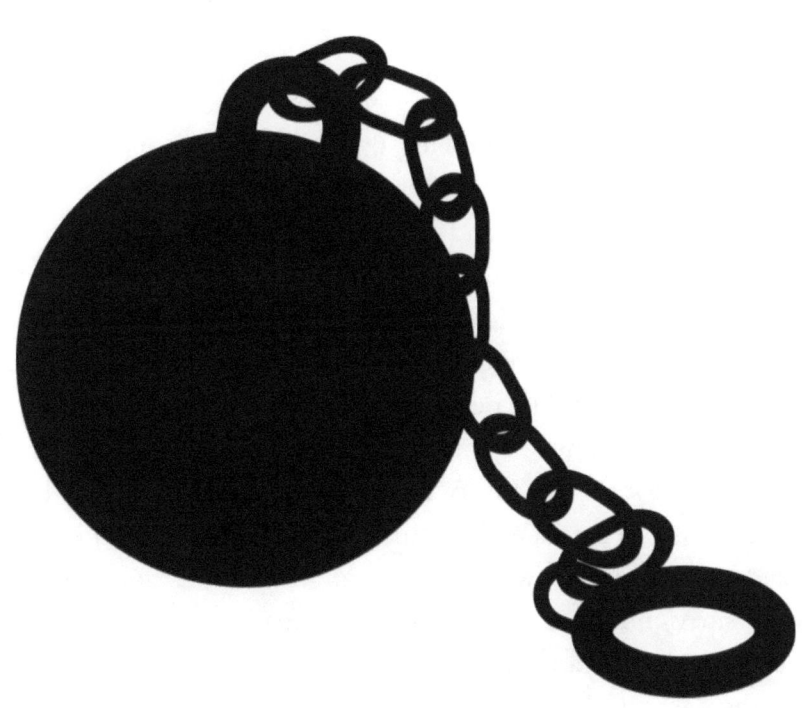

Praying against Addictions

Word of Encouragement

Dear Friend,

As you lift your prayers for your loved ones struggling with addiction, take heart in knowing that you are walking a path of profound hope and compassion. Your earnest prayers are a testament to your love and faith, and they hold tremendous power. Trust in the unchanging promises of God, who is ever-present and fully capable of bringing healing and restoration. Remember that He listens to every prayer and will respond in ways that align with His perfect plan.

In moments of uncertainty, lean on the truth that God's grace is more than enough to cover every challenge, and His love never fails. Even when the journey seems long and the road ahead is difficult, know that His strength upholds you and His peace surrounds you. Keep your faith steadfast and your heart open, for God's transformative power is at work, bringing light into the darkest places.

With unwavering hope and encouragement.

Praying against Addictions

Our Dear Heavenly Father,

I come before You today with a sincere heart, seeking Your intervention in my own battle against addiction. Lord, I acknowledge that this struggle is not merely against flesh and blood but against the spiritual forces of darkness, as Ephesians 6:12 (NIV) reminds us: "Our struggle is not against flesh and blood, but against the rulers, against the authorities, against the powers of this dark world and against the spiritual forces of evil in the heavenly realms." I pray earnestly that You would break the chains of addiction in my life and remove the evil desires that bind me.

Father, Your Word assures me in Psalm 86:15 (NIV), "But you, Lord, are a compassionate and gracious God, slow to anger, abounding in love and faithfulness." I ask You to purify my body with Your cleansing blood and heal me from the destructive effects of addiction. Grant me the wisdom, patience, and strength I need to pursue recovery and wholeness. Help me to love myself as You love me, guiding me back onto the path of restoration.

Lord, Your promise in Isaiah 9:2 (NIV) brings me hope: "The people walking in darkness have seen a great light; on those living in the land of deep darkness a light has dawned." I pray that You would shine Your divine light into the darkness of addiction, breaking its hold over me. Strengthen me in moments of temptation and let me find refuge and strength in You alone, as Psalm 46:1 (NIV) assures: "God is our refuge and strength, an ever-present help in trouble."

Father, I recognise that I cannot overcome this on my own. I seek Your forgiveness and divine assistance, relying on the truth of Philippians 4:13 (NIV): "I can do all this through him who gives me strength." Help me to live a life that honours You, finding true joy and fulfilment in my relationship with You rather than in worldly pleasures. Enable me to stand firm on Your promises and to trust in Your power to deliver me.

I also lift up my loved ones who are struggling with addiction. Lord, I intercede for them, asking that You would break their chains and remove their desires for substances or behaviours that enslave them. Purify their bodies and heal them from the effects of addiction, and grant us, their family members, the wisdom and strength to support them on their journey. Help us to love them as You love them, guiding them back to wholeness and restoration.

As we all fix our eyes on You, I trust that our help comes from You alone, as Psalm 121:2 (NIV) says: "My help comes from the Lord, the Maker of heaven and earth." I thank You in advance for the healing and transformation You will bring into our lives. May we find strength and refuge in Your presence, trusting in Your ability to renew and restore.

In Jesus' precious name, I pray,
Amen.

Verse

Deuteronomy 20:4

"For the Lord your God is the one who goes with you to fight for you against your enemies to give you victory."

✯✯✯

Prayer moves mountains, breaks chains, and brings healing. Trust in God's power to deliver and restore.

Daily Reflection

Prayer for Mourning and Grieving

Word of Encouragement

Dear friend,

As you lift your heart in prayer during this time of mourning, remember that you are not alone. The Lord, who promises comfort to those who mourn, is with you every step of the way (Matthew 5:4). Your prayers are heard, and your grief is known to Him who collects every tear. Take comfort in His presence and the assurance that He understands your pain intimately.

May you find strength in His Word, peace in His promises, and solace in His unfailing love. Keep leaning on Him, for He is your refuge and strength in this season of sorrow.

With prayers for peace and healing.

Prayer for Mourning and Grieving

Our Dear Heavenly Father,

In the midst of deep sorrow and grief, I come before You, knowing You are the God of all comfort and compassion (Psalm 34:18). Your Word assures me that You are close to the brokenhearted and save those who are crushed in spirit (Psalm 34:18). I lift up my heartache and pain to You, knowing that You collect my tears in Your bottle and record each one in Your book (Psalm 56:8).

Jesus, You wept with those who mourned (John 11:35), understanding grief intimately. I ask for Your gentle touch upon my life, helping me to process this loss with honesty and vulnerability before You.

Holy Spirit, be my counsellor and Comforter during this time of mourning. Guide my thoughts and emotions, bringing peace to my troubled heart. Your Word promises that those who mourn will be comforted (Matthew 5:4). I cling to this promise and ask for Your supernatural peace to fill my soul.

Father, grant me strength to face each day. Give me the courage to grieve honestly and the grace to lean on You for support. Help me find solace in Your presence and in the love of those around me who care deeply.

I surrender my pain and sorrow into Your loving hands. You are my refuge and strength, a very present help in times of trouble (Psalm 46:1). Surround me with Your love and grant me the resilience to walk through this season of mourning with hope in You.

Thank You, Father, for Your unwavering love and compassion. May Your peace, which surpasses all understanding, guard my heart and mind in Christ Jesus (Philippians 4:7).

Lord, today I ask You to embrace me as my heart overflows with grief and unanswered questions. You said, "Blessed are those who mourn, for they will be comforted." Lift my eyes to catch a glimpse of eternity and be comforted by the promise of heaven.

Give me hope in my confusion and grace to live in thanksgiving to You. Help me cherish all the good memories and find joy and peace through Your Holy Spirit. Comfort my family, unite our hearts, and help us find strength in our loss.

Draw close to me, Lord, and rescue me from this pain and grief. Let me find strength and peace in Your presence. Even as I am consumed with sorrow, I thank You for Your promises. You renew the strength of those who hope in You; they soar on wings like eagles, run and do not grow weary, walk and do not faint (Isaiah 40:31).

Father, in this difficult time, help me find comfort, peace, and strength in You. Be with me every hour of every day. Though I walk through the darkest valley, I will fear no evil, for You are with me; Your rod and Your staff, they comfort me (Psalm 23:4).

Amidst my pain and questions, I find peace knowing that to be absent from this body is to be present with the Lord. Thank You for this assurance that we will meet again.

Heavenly Father, wrap Your loving arms around me when waves of grief threaten to overcome me. Sustain me with Your love and mercy. Be my refuge and stronghold through this difficult time. Watch over me and grant me strength each day.

Hear my prayers, O Lord, and comfort me in this unbearable loss. Help me find strength and peace in Your presence. I bring my sorrows, grief, and pain to You, knowing that You carry them all. Thank You, Lord, for the privilege of prayer, where I can bring everything to You.

In Jesus' precious name, I pray.

Amen.

Verse

Matthew 5:4

"Blessed are those who mourn, for they will be comforted."

✧✧✧

In times of mourning, may God's comforting presence embrace you, turning sorrow into hope and tears into peace.

Daily Reflection

Prayer to Unleash Miracles and Blessings over My Life

Word of Encouragement

Dear Friend,

In times like these, when we seek miracles and blessings, it's easy to feel overwhelmed or uncertain. But I want to remind you of something important—God is faithful. He hears our prayers, knows our hearts, and His promises never fail.

Remember, "With God all things are possible" (Matthew 19:26). This verse has been a source of strength for me, especially when facing challenges or waiting for answers. It reminds me that even in the midst of uncertainty, God is working behind the scenes, orchestrating His perfect plan for us.

So, as you continue to pray and seek God's guidance, hold on to your faith. Trust that He is listening, and His timing is always perfect. Your persistence in prayer is a testament to your faith in His goodness and love.

Take care and may God's peace and grace surround you abundantly.

Blessings.

Prayer to Unleash Miracles and Blessings over My Life

Our Dear Heavenly Father,

I come before You in humble reverence, acknowledging Your sovereignty and goodness. Your Word declares that nothing is impossible for You, and that You delight in blessing Your children abundantly. Today, I boldly ask for Your miraculous intervention and abundant blessings to overflow in my life.

Lord, You are the God who performs miracles and wonders. Your power knows no bounds, and Your love for me is endless (Psalm 77:14). I surrender my life into Your hands, trusting that Your plans for me are good and filled with hope (Jeremiah 29:11). Open the floodgates of heaven and pour out Your blessings upon me according to Your riches in glory (Philippians 4:19).

Father, I pray for miraculous provision in every area of my life—spiritually, emotionally, physically, and financially. You are my provider, and I trust in Your provision as I seek first Your kingdom and Your righteousness (Matthew 6:33). Grant me wisdom and discernment to recognise Your blessings and opportunities as they come.

Lord Jesus, You are the same yesterday, today, and forever (Hebrews 13:8). Just as You performed miracles during Your earthly ministry, I believe You are working miracles in my life even now. Heal where there is sickness, mend what is broken, and bring restoration where there is loss.

Holy Spirit, guide my steps and lead me in paths of righteousness. Strengthen my faith and help me to walk in obedience to Your Word. May Your presence be a constant source of comfort and assurance, knowing that You are working all things together for my good (Romans 8:28).

Father, I pray for miracles that will glorify Your name and testify to Your greatness. Let Your light shine brightly through me, so that others may see Your works and come to know You as their Savior and Redeemer.

Thank You, Lord, for hearing my prayer and for the miracles and blessings that are already on their way. I surrender my desires to Your perfect will, confident that You will exceed my expectations and do exceedingly abundantly above all that I ask or think (Ephesians 3:20).

In Jesus' mighty name,
Amen.

Verse

Ephesians 3:20-21

> *"Now to him who is able to do immeasurably more than all we ask or imagine, according to His power that is at work within us, to him be glory in the church and in Christ Jesus throughout all generations, forever and ever! Amen."*

✭ ✭ ✭

Open your heart to God's limitless power, where miracles and blessings overflow beyond imagination.

Daily Reflection

A Powerful Prayer over Anger, Resentment and Bitterness

Word of Encouragement

Dear Friend,

As you lift your heart in prayer to release anger, resentment, and bitterness, know that you are taking a powerful step towards healing and restoration. God sees your sincerity and is faithful to answer prayers that align with His will. Trust in His promise to transform your heart and bring peace where there is turmoil. Stay strong in faith, for His grace is sufficient, and His love will guide you through. Keep seeking His presence, and may His peace fill you abundantly.

With hope and encouragement.

A Powerful Prayer over Anger, Resentment and Bitterness

Our Dear Heavenly Father,

Today, I stand before You in awe of Your greatness and boundless love. Your Word teaches us that anger does not bring about the righteous life that You desire (James 1:20). Today, I bring before You the struggles I have with anger, resentment, and bitterness in my heart. Lord, I confess these feelings to You and ask for Your forgiveness and cleansing.

Father, Your Word also tells us to get rid of all bitterness, rage and anger, brawling and slander, along with every form of malice. Help me to let go of these negative emotions that weigh heavily on my heart. Replace them with Your peace that surpasses all understanding (Ephesians 4:31; Philippians 4:7).

Lord Jesus, You are our ultimate example of grace and forgiveness. You forgave those who crucified You, saying, "Father, forgive them, for they do not know what they are doing" (Luke 23:34). Teach me to forgive others as You have forgiven me. Give me a heart that reflects Your love and mercy.

Holy Spirit, empower me to control my reactions and responses. Your Word encourages us to be quick to listen, slow to speak, and slow to become angry (James 1:19). Grant me the wisdom and self-control to manage my emotions in a way that honours You.

Father, I pray for healing in relationships that have been strained by my anger and bitterness. Help me to reconcile where possible and to extend grace and forgiveness where needed. May Your love flow through me, touching the lives of those around me.

Thank You, Lord, for Your patience and unfailing love towards me. Thank You for the freedom I find in surrendering my hurts and grievances to You. I trust in Your promise that if we confess our sins, You are faithful and just and will forgive us our sins and purify us from all unrighteousness (1 John 1:9).

Father, fill me afresh with Your Spirit, that I may walk in the fruit of the Spirit—love, joy, peace, patience, kindness, goodness, faithfulness, gentleness, and self-control (Galatians 5:22-23). Help me to live a life that reflects Your grace and mercy, bringing glory to Your name.

In Jesus' precious name, I pray,

Amen.

Verse

Ephesians 4:31-32

> *"Let all bitterness, wrath, anger, clamour, and evil speaking be put away from you, with all malice. And be kind to one another, tender-hearted, forgiving one another, even as God in Christ forgave you."*

✶ ✶ ✶

Let go of anger and bitterness, embrace God's peace, and extend forgiveness as He forgave you.

Daily Reflection

Praying for Children Who are Missing

Word of Encouragement

Dear Friend,

Your heartfelt prayer for the missing children and their families is a testament to your deep compassion and faith in God's power and goodness. Your words echo with hope and trust in His ability to bring comfort, protection, and restoration. Your commitment to intercede on behalf of others in their time of need is truly inspiring.

In moments like these, where the heartache of others weighs heavily, your prayers serve as a beacon of light and hope. Your faithfulness in seeking God's intervention reflects His love shining through you, offering strength to those who are suffering and believing for miracles.

Continue to hold fast to God's promises, knowing that He hears every prayer offered with a sincere heart. Your prayers are making a difference, bringing comfort and peace to those who need it most. May God bless you abundantly for your compassionate spirit and unwavering faith.

With prayers and encouragement.

Praying for Children that are Missing

Our Dear Heavenly Father,

Today, with hearts heavy yet hopeful, we lift up to You the children who are missing and their families who are enduring the anguish of their absence. Your Word assures us that You are close to the broken-hearted and that You rescue those who are crushed in spirit (Psalm 34:18). We entrust these precious children into Your loving care.

Lord Jesus, during Your earthly ministry, You embraced children and declared that the kingdom of heaven belongs to them (Matthew 19:14). We ask You to surround these missing children with Your protection. Send Your angels to guard them, wherever they may be, and lead them safely back to the embrace of their loved ones.

Holy Spirit, Comforter and counsellor, we pray for the families who are enduring this unimaginable pain. Bring them peace that surpasses understanding (Philippians 4:7) and sustain them with Your unfailing strength. May they find refuge in Your presence amidst the uncertainty.

Father, we lift up all those involved in the search and rescue efforts. Grant wisdom and discernment to law enforcement, volunteers, and every individual tirelessly working to bring these children home safely. Guide their efforts and lead them in the right paths (Psalm 23:3).

Lord, You are the God who hears our prayers and answers according to Your perfect will. We plead for miracles and divine interventions in these distressing circumstances. Let Your light pierce through the darkness and bring hope where there is despair.

We stand firm on Your promises, Lord, knowing that nothing is impossible with You (Luke 1:37). Uphold these children in Your arms of love and swiftly reunite them with their families. May Your name be glorified through the restoration and healing that You bring.

In Jesus' precious name, I pray,
Amen.

Verse

Mark 10:14

"Let the little children come to me, and do not hinder them, for the kingdom of God belongs to such as these."

✯✯✯

Pray with hope, for God hears our cries and moves in powerful ways to bring comfort, protection, and restoration.

Daily Reflection

Prayer for my Children During Exams

Word of Encouragement

Dear Friend,

As you pray fervently for your children during their exams, remember the assurance found in Proverbs 16:3: "Commit your work to the Lord, and your plans will be established." This verse reminds us that when we entrust our efforts to God, He faithfully establishes our paths and guides us through every challenge.

Philippians 4:6-7 encourages us further: "Do not be anxious about anything, but in every situation, by prayer and petition, with thanksgiving, present your requests to God. And the peace of God, which transcends all understanding, will guard your hearts and your minds in Christ Jesus." As you pray for your children, pour out your heart to God with thanksgiving, knowing that His peace will surround and protect them.

Isaiah 41:10 declares, "So do not fear, for I am with you; do not be dismayed, for I am your God. I will strengthen you and help you; I will uphold you with my righteous right hand." God promises His presence and strength to those who trust in Him. Let this truth comfort and strengthen you as you intercede for your children's success and well-being.

Commit every concern to the Lord, knowing that He cares deeply for you and your children (1 Peter 5:7). Your prayers are powerful and effective (James 5:16), and God hears every word spoken in faith (Mark 11:24). Keep standing firm in prayer, trusting that God is working all things together for good (Romans 8:28).

May God bless you abundantly as you continue to seek His guidance and provision.

Stay strong in faith.

Prayer for My Children During Exams

Our Dear Heavenly Father,

I come before You overflowing with gratitude for the precious gift of my children, whom You have entrusted to my care. As they prepare to face their exams, I lift them up to You, knowing that You are their strength and refuge in times of need.

Father, Your Word assures us that if we lack wisdom, we should ask You, who gives generously without finding fault (James 1:5). Grant my children wisdom beyond their years, clarity of thought, and the ability to recall all they have studied. Equip them with knowledge and understanding as they approach their exams, filling their hearts with confidence in Your provision.

Lord, You have promised to be with us wherever we go and to never leave us nor forsake us (Joshua 1:9). I ask for Your tangible presence to surround my children during their exams. Calm their nerves, Lord, and grant them Your peace that surpasses all understanding (Philippians 4:7). Let them feel Your loving embrace and assurance throughout this challenging time.

Lord Jesus, You are the Prince of Peace, and Your peace guards our hearts and minds. I pray that Your peace will reign in their hearts, keeping them focused and free from anxiety (John 14:27). Help them to trust in Your plan for their lives, knowing that You hold their future securely in Your hands.

Holy Spirit, You are our counsellor and Helper, guiding us into all truth (John 16:13). I ask You to come alongside my children as they prepare and during their exams. Remind them of all they have studied, bring to their remembrance everything they need to excel, and grant them clarity and understanding as they answer each question.

Father, I also pray for physical strength and endurance for

my children during this demanding period. Grant them good health and vitality so that they may perform to the best of their abilities, bringing glory to Your name.

Thank You, Lord, for hearing my heartfelt prayer. I commit my children into Your loving care, trusting that You will guide them through this season with Your wisdom and grace. May their achievements bring honour to Your name and serve as a testament to Your faithfulness.

In Jesus' name,
Amen.

Verse

Proverbs 16:3

"Commit your work to the Lord, and your plans will be established."

✯✯✯

Pray with confidence, entrusting your children's exams to God, knowing His peace will guard and guide them through every challenge.

Daily Reflection

Prayer for our World

Word of Encouragement

Dear Friend,

As you pray for our world, remember that your prayers are powerful and meaningful. God hears every word you speak on behalf of others and honours your heart's desire for peace, justice, and healing. Your faithfulness in prayer brings hope in a world often filled with chaos. Trust that God's love and sovereignty extend over all situations. Your prayers make a difference, and God works through you to fulfil His purposes on earth.

The passage from 1 Timothy 2:1-2 emphasises the importance of praying for all people, including those in authority. It encourages us to offer petitions, intercession, and thanksgiving. Petitions are specific requests for God's intervention, intercession involves praying on behalf of others, and thanksgiving acknowledges God's faithfulness. These prayers aim for peaceful and righteous living, reflecting our desire for God's will to prevail on earth.

With gratitude for your compassion and faith.

Prayer for our World

Our Dear Heavenly Father,

We approach Your throne with humble hearts, acknowledging that You are the sovereign Lord who holds all nations and peoples in Your hands (Psalm 47:7-8). Today, we intercede for our world, guided by Your Word that instructs us to pray for our leaders and seek peace among all peoples (1 Timothy 2:1-2).

Lord Jesus, You are the Prince of Peace, and Your kingdom brings reconciliation and healing (Isaiah 9:6). We pray earnestly for peace to reign where there is conflict and strife, and for Your light to dispel darkness and despair (John 8:12).

Father, You are just and righteous in all Your ways (Isaiah 30:18). We lift up the cries for justice where there is oppression and inequality, asking for Your intervention and guidance in these matters.

Holy Spirit, Comforter and Advocate, we seek Your presence among the suffering and marginalised (John 14:16). Bring comfort to the broken-hearted and healing to the wounded. May Your love and compassion shine forth in our world.

Father, Your desire is for all people to come to know You and be saved (1 Timothy 2:4). We pray for the spread of the Gospel, that hearts would be opened to receive Your grace and truth.

We entrust our leaders into Your hands, praying for wisdom and discernment as they make decisions impacting our world (Proverbs 21:1). Guide them in paths of righteousness and lead them to seek Your will in all things.

Thank You, Father, for hearing our prayers. We trust in Your unfailing love and power to bring about Your purposes in our world. May Your kingdom come, and Your will be done on earth as it is in heaven.

    In Jesus' precious name, I pray,
    Amen.

Verse

1 Timothy 2:1-2

> *"I urge, then, first of all, that petitions, prayers, intercession and thanksgiving be made for all people— for kings and all those in authority, that we may live peaceful and quiet lives in all godliness and holiness."*

✵ ✵ ✵

Let us pray fervently for our world, trusting in God's power to bring peace, justice, and healing to every corner of the earth.

Daily Reflection

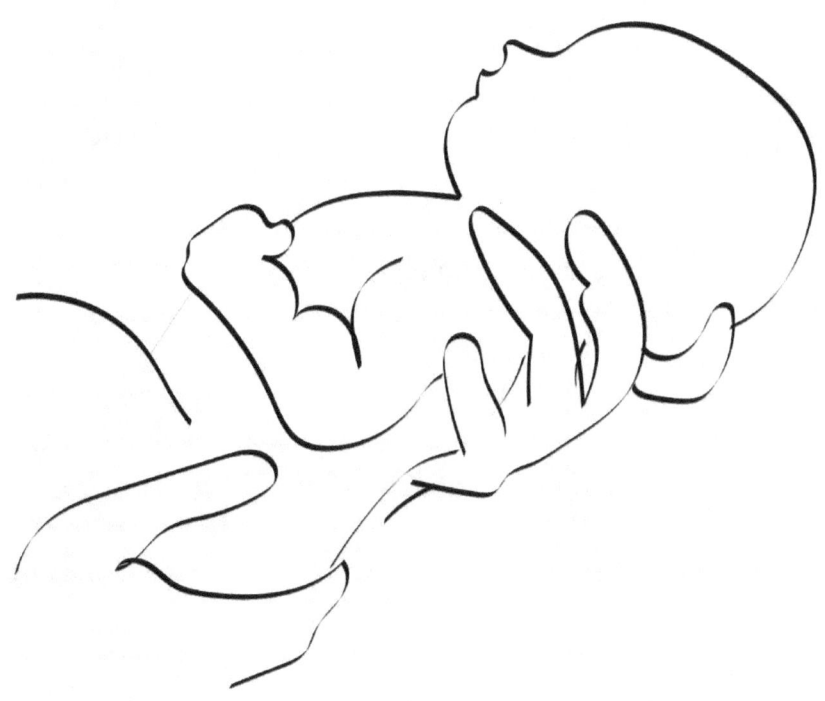

Prayer for Women Seeking the Gift of Motherhood

Word of Encouragement

Dear Friend,

As you continue to trust in God's perfect timing and plan for your life, I want to encourage you with these words from Scripture. God's love for you is immeasurable, and His promises are sure. Remember, He who created the heavens and the earth is the same God who knit you together in your mother's womb (Psalm 139:13). He knows your heart's desires and holds your future in His hands.

In moments of doubt or longing, hold onto His promise in Isaiah 44:2, "This is what the Lord says— he who made you, who formed you in the womb, and who will help you." God's promises are not just words on a page but a testament to His faithfulness and unchanging nature. He is with you, walking beside you through every step of this journey.

Keep your heart steadfast, trusting in His goodness and timing. The Lord is your refuge and strength, a very present help in trouble (Psalm 46:1). Let His peace, which surpasses all understanding, guard your heart and mind (Philippians 4:7). Know that you are never alone; God's love surrounds you, and His grace is sufficient for you (2 Corinthians 12:9).

Your faith is a powerful testament to God's work in your life. As you continue to pray and seek His will, let your hope be anchored in His promises. He is faithful to complete the good work He has begun in you (Philippians 1:6).

May you find strength and encouragement in His Word today, and may your heart be filled with the peace that only God can provide. You are deeply loved and cherished by the Creator of the universe, who is always with you.

With love and prayers.

Prayer for Women Seeking the Gift of Motherhood

Our Dear Heavenly Father,

I come before You with a heart full of hope and longing, trusting in Your perfect timing and sovereignty over all things. You are the giver of life, and You knit each of us together in our mother's womb (Psalm 139:13). I thank You for the deep desire for motherhood that You have placed in my heart.

Lord, Your Word assures us that children are a heritage from You, a reward, and a blessing (Psalm 127:3). I lift up my earnest desire to become a mother, knowing that You are the One who opens and closes the womb (Genesis 30:22). I surrender my hopes, fears, and uncertainties to You, trusting that Your plans for me are good, to prosper me and not to harm me, to give me hope and a future (Jeremiah 29:11).

Father, I ask for Your grace and strength to sustain me through this journey. Grant me patience to wait upon You, and courage to face each day with unwavering faith in Your promises. Help me to find peace and contentment in Your presence, knowing that Your timing is perfect, and Your ways are higher than mine (Isaiah 55:8-9).

Lord Jesus, You are the Healer and the Restorer of all things. I pray for Your touch upon my body, that You would bring wholeness and fertility according to Your will. May Your healing power flow through me, restoring any brokenness and preparing me for the precious gift of motherhood.

Holy Spirit, comforter and guide, fill my heart with Your peace that surpasses all understanding (Philippians 4:7). Strengthen my faith and help me to trust in Your faithfulness, even in moments of doubt or discouragement. Let Your love surround me and remind me that You are with me every step of this journey.

Father, I also pray for wisdom and discernment as I seek medical advice and explore options. Guide the hands of the healthcare professionals who are supporting me and grant them insight into the best course of action for my well-being.

Above all, Lord, may Your will be done in my life. I surrender my desires to You, knowing that You are able to do immeasurably more than all I ask or imagine, according to Your power that is at work within me (Ephesians 3:20).

Thank You, Father, for hearing my prayer. I place my hope and trust in You, knowing that You are faithful to fulfil Your promises. May Your name be glorified through the miracle of new life, and may I be a witness to Your goodness and grace.

In Jesus' precious name, I pray,

Amen.

Verse

Psalm 127:3 (NIV)

"Children are a heritage from the Lord, offspring a reward from him."

✼✼✼

God's timing is perfect, His promises are sure, and His love for you is unfailing. May your faith in His plan bring peace and strength as you await the blessings He has prepared for you.

Daily Reflection

A Prayer for Discovering and Using Gifts and Talents

Word of Encouragement

Dear Friend,

As you reflect on the parable of the talents and the encouragement it offers, remember that God has uniquely gifted you with talents and abilities. He delights in seeing you use them for His glory and the benefit of others. Stay faithful and diligent in cultivating these gifts, knowing that even small beginnings can lead to significant impact when entrusted to God. Keep seeking His guidance and wisdom, and trust that He will multiply your efforts beyond what you can imagine. May you continue to walk in His joy and fulfil His purposes with confidence.

Blessings to you as you journey in faith.

A Prayer for Discovering and Using Gifts and Talents

Our Dear Heavenly Father,

I approach Your throne with a heart full of gratitude for the unique gifts and talents You have graciously bestowed upon me. Your Word teaches us that each of us has received special gifts from You for the common good (1 Corinthians 12:7). I pray that You would help me recognise, develop, and utilise these gifts according to Your will.

Lord, You are the source of all good gifts, and every perfect gift comes from You (James 1:17). I thank You for entrusting me with talents that reflect Your creativity and wisdom. Grant me the discernment and courage to use these gifts effectively for Your glory and the benefit of others.

Father, You have created me in Your image and called me by name (Isaiah 43:1). I ask for Your guidance in discovering the full extent of my gifts and talents. Help me to cultivate them diligently and to steward them wisely, so that they may bear fruit that honours You.

Lord Jesus, You are the perfect example of using gifts and talents to serve others. You humbly served and sacrificed for the sake of humanity, demonstrating love in its purest form (Philippians 2:5-8). May Your life inspire me to use my gifts selflessly and compassionately.

Holy Spirit, You empower and equip Your people with various gifts for the building up of the body of Christ (1 Corinthians 12:4-6). Fill me with Your presence and wisdom as I discern how to best use my gifts in my daily life, in my community, and in Your kingdom.

Father, I commit my gifts and talents into Your hands. May they be a reflection of Your grace and a testament to Your faithfulness. Use me as an instrument of Your peace and love in a world that needs Your light.

Thank You, Lord, for the privilege of serving You with the gifts You have given me. May I always seek Your will and glorify Your name through the use of my talents. May Your Spirit continue to lead and guide me on this journey of discovery and service.

In Jesus' precious name, I pray,
Amen.

Verse

Matthew 25:21 (NIV)

> *"His master replied, 'Well done, good and faithful servant! You have been faithful with a few things; I will put you in charge of many things. Come and share your master's happiness!'"*

✧ ✧ ✧

> *Discovering and using our gifts and talents is a journey of faithfulness and stewardship, leading to meaningful impact and sharing in God's joy.*

Daily Reflection

A Prayer for Forgiveness

Word of Encouragement

Dear Friend,

In moments of seeking forgiveness and reconciliation, remember the words from 1 John 1:9: "If we confess our sins, he is faithful and just and will forgive us our sins and purify us from all unrighteousness." Take heart in knowing that through genuine repentance, God eagerly extends His forgiveness and restores us with His loving grace. May you find peace and assurance in His promise of redemption.

With hope and encouragement.

A Prayer for Forgiveness

Our Dear Heavenly Father,

I come before You with a heart burdened by my sins, knowing that I have fallen short of Your glory (Romans 3:23). I confess my sins to You and ask for Your forgiveness. Your Word assures us that if we confess our sins, You are faithful and just to forgive us and to cleanse us from all unrighteousness (1 John 1:9). Thank You, Father, for Your unfailing love and mercy.

Lord Jesus, You bore the punishment for my sins on the cross, and through Your sacrifice, I am redeemed and forgiven (Ephesians 1:7). I ask for Your precious blood to cleanse me from all guilt and shame. Wash me thoroughly from my iniquity and cleanse me from my sin (Psalm 51:2). Renew a steadfast spirit within me and restore to me the joy of Your salvation (Psalm 51:10, 12).

Father, forgive me for the times I have turned away from You and chosen my own way. Forgive me for the hurt I have caused others and for the ways I have failed to love as You love. Create in me a clean heart, O God, and renew a right spirit within me (Psalm 51:10).

Holy Spirit, convict me of any sin that I need to confess and repent of. Help me to walk in Your ways, to live a life that honours You, and to bear fruit worthy of repentance (Matthew 3:8). Lead me in paths of righteousness for Your name's sake (Psalm 23:3).

Thank You, Lord, for Your boundless grace and forgiveness. May Your mercy flow through me to others, as I extend forgiveness to those who have wronged me (Ephesians 4:32). Help me to forgive as You have forgiven me.

I surrender myself completely to You, Lord. Fill me with Your peace and assurance of Your forgiveness. May Your love and grace transform my life, that I may live in obedience to Your will and bring glory to Your name.

In Jesus' precious name, I pray,
Amen.

Verse

1 John 1:9

> *"If we confess our sins, he is faithful and just to forgive us our sins and to cleanse us from all unrighteousness."*

✧✧✧

Through repentance and confession, God's boundless grace cleanses and renews, bringing peace and restoration.

Daily Reflection

A Prayer for Overcoming Fear

Word of Encouragement

Dear Friend,

As you lift your prayers to God, remember that He has given you a spirit of power, love, and self-control (2 Timothy 1:7). In moments of fear, His strength sustains you, His love surrounds you, and His Spirit guides you. Trust in His promises, knowing that He is with you every step of the way. Take courage, for through Him, you can overcome any fear that may assail you.

May you find peace in His presence and strength in His Word as you walk in faith and boldness.

Blessings to you.

A Prayer for Overcoming Fear

Our Dear Heavenly Father,

I come before You with a heart weighed down by fear, but I know Your Word assures me that You have not given us a spirit of fear, but of power, love, and a sound mind (2 Timothy 1:7). Lord, I confess that fear has gripped my heart and mind, but I choose to trust in Your promises today.

Lord Jesus, You have commanded us not to be anxious about anything, but in everything, by prayer and petition, with thanksgiving, to present our requests to You. So now, I bring before You all my fears and worries, asking for Your peace that surpasses all understanding to guard my heart and mind in Christ Jesus (Philippians 4:6-7).

Holy Spirit, You are my Comforter and Counsellor. I ask for Your presence to fill me and dispel every fear that seeks to paralyse me. Help me to walk in faith, knowing that You are with me always, even to the end of the age (Matthew 28:20).

Father, I pray that You would strengthen my faith and help me to focus on Your truth. Your Word says, "When I am afraid, I put my trust in You" (Psalm 56:3). I choose to trust in You completely, knowing that You are my refuge and strength, an ever-present help in trouble (Psalm 46:1).

Lord, I surrender my fears and anxieties to You. Replace them with Your peace that transcends all circumstances. Help me to fix my eyes on Jesus, the author and perfecter of my faith, who endured the cross for the joy set before Him (Hebrews 12:2).

Thank You, Lord, for Your faithfulness and love that cast out all fear (1 John 4:18). May Your perfect love continue to abide in me, driving out every fear and filling me with Your peace.

In Jesus' precious name, I pray,
Amen.

Verse

2 Timothy 1:7 (ESV)

"For God gave us a spirit not of fear but of power and love and self-control."

✯✯✯

Trust in God's power, love, and guidance to overcome fear and walk in peace.

Daily Reflection

A Prayer for Compassion

Word of Encouragement

Dear Friend,

Your heart for the poor and needy mirrors God's own compassion for the marginalised and vulnerable. Remember the words of Proverbs 19:17, 'Whoever is kind to the poor lends to the LORD, and he will reward them for what they have done.' Your prayers and acts of kindness are not in vain; they are seeds sown in fertile soil, destined to bear fruit in God's perfect time. Continue to trust in His provision and guidance as you reach out to those in need. Your compassion is a testament to His love working through you.

May His promise encourage and strengthen you, and may you continue to be a beacon of hope and compassion in this world.

In Christ's love.

A Prayer for Compassion

Our Dear Heavenly Father,

I come before You humbly, recognising Your abundant compassion and mercy toward us. Your Word teaches us to be compassionate, just as You are compassionate (Luke 6:36). Lord, fill my heart with Your love and compassion, that I may see others as You see them and act with kindness and empathy.

Father, help me to understand the struggles and pains of those around me (Romans 12:15). May Your compassion move me to action, to comfort those who are hurting and to extend a helping hand to those in need (Isaiah 58:10).

Lord Jesus, You showed compassion to the weary and the broken-hearted (Matthew 9:36). Teach me to follow Your example, to reach out to the marginalised, and to bring healing and hope wherever I go.

Holy Spirit, guide me in showing compassion not only in words but also in deeds (1 John 3:18). Help me to listen attentively, to speak words of encouragement, and to share Your love with everyone I meet.

Father, grant me a heart that is quick to forgive and slow to judge (Colossians 3:12-13). May Your compassion overflow from me, touching lives and bringing glory to Your name.

Thank You, Lord, for Your boundless compassion toward us. May I reflect Your love and compassion in all I do, for the honour and glory of Your Kingdom.

In Jesus' precious name, I pray,
Amen.

Verse

Proverbs 19:17

> *"Whoever is kind to the poor lends to the Lord, and he will reward them for what they have done."*

✣ ✣ ✣

Compassion is the reflection of God's love in action, transforming hearts and lives with grace.

Daily Reflection

A Prayer for Unity and Harmony in Family

Word of Encouragement

Dear Friend,

As you seek unity and harmony within your family, remember the words of Psalm 133:1, 'Behold, how good and pleasant it is when brothers dwell in unity!' Your commitment to nurturing love and understanding among your loved ones reflects God's heart for His people. Trust in His guidance and grace as you navigate the joys and challenges of family life. May His peace fill your home and His wisdom guide every decision you make.

With prayers for continued blessings and unity in your family.

A Prayer Unity and Harmony in Family

Our Dear Heavenly Father,

We come before You today, seeking Your guidance and grace for our family. Your Word teaches us in Psalm 133:1, "Behold, how good and pleasant it is when brothers dwell in unity!" Lord, we desire unity and harmony in our family according to Your will.

Father, help us to love one another deeply, as You have loved us (John 13:34). Grant us the humility to serve each other with compassion and patience, bearing with one another in love (Ephesians 4:2). Strengthen our bonds of affection and understanding, that we may honour and respect each family member as a gift from You.

Lord Jesus, You prayed for unity among Your followers, that they may be one as You and the Father are one (John 17:21). We ask for Your presence to fill our home with peace, casting out any discord or division. May Your Spirit guide our words and actions, leading us in paths of righteousness and reconciliation.

Holy Spirit, empower us to forgive one another as You have forgiven us (Colossians 3:13). Help us to bear each other's burdens and share in each other's joys, building up our family in faith and love. Let Your fruit – love, joy, peace, patience, kindness, goodness, faithfulness, gentleness, and self-control – abound in our relationships (Galatians 5:22-23).

Father, we commit our family into Your loving hands. Give us wisdom to resolve conflicts peacefully and discernment to nurture a home filled with Your presence. May our family be a beacon of Your light and love, drawing others to know You through our unity and harmony.

Thank You, Lord, for Your faithfulness to hear our prayers. We trust in Your promises to bless those who dwell in unity, and

we ask for Your continual grace to abide with us.
 In Jesus' precious name, I pray,
 Amen.

Verse

Psalm 133:1 (NIV)

"Behold, how good and pleasant it is when God's people live together in unity!"

✫✫✫

May our family be a testament to God's love, where unity flourishes and harmony abounds.

Daily Reflection

Prayer for Activating the Fruit of the Spirit

Word of Encouragement

Dear Friend,

As you embrace the Fruit of the Spirit in your daily life, remember that you are on a remarkable journey of growth and transformation. The path you are walking is one of deepening your connection with God and reflecting His character in all that you do. The attributes of love, joy, peace, patience, kindness, goodness, faithfulness, gentleness, and self-control are not just qualities to aspire to—they are the very essence of the life that God desires for you.

As you pray and seek to embody these virtues, know that you are not alone. The Holy Spirit is your guide, your strength, and your helper. When you feel challenged or find it difficult to live out these attributes, remember the promises of God's Word. He has equipped you with His Spirit to manifest these qualities, and He is faithful to complete the good work He has begun in you.

Your efforts to cultivate these virtues will not go unnoticed. Each step you take towards living out the Fruit of the Spirit is a testament to God's transformative power in your life. You are a beacon of His love and grace, shining brightly in a world that needs His light.

Be encouraged by the knowledge that your growth in these attributes is a reflection of God's love and His work within you. As you continue to seek Him and apply His Word, you are becoming more like Christ and making a difference in the lives of those around you.

Keep pressing forward with faith and confidence, trusting in God's promises and the guidance of the Holy Spirit. Your journey is one of continuous transformation, and with each day, you are growing closer to the person God created you to be.

Fruit of the Spirit are Love, Joy, Peace, Patience, Kindness, Goodness, Faithfulness, Gentleness, Self-Control

In His love and grace.

Prayer for Activating the Fruit of the Spirit

Our Dear Heavenly Father,

I come before You today with a heart open to Your guidance, earnestly seeking to live a life that honours You and reflects Your love. Your Word in Galatians 5:22-23 reminds us of the attributes that should flow from a life led by Your Holy Spirit. As I strive to embody these qualities, I ask for Your divine help to manifest them in my life.

Lord, fill me with Your love—a love that mirrors the profound, sacrificial love You have shown me. As You commanded in John 13:34: "A new command I give you: Love one another. As I have loved you, so you must love one another." May Your love overflow in my heart, guiding my interactions and shaping my relationships with others.

Grant me joy that transcends all circumstances, as described in Philippians 4:4: "Rejoice in the Lord always. I will say it again: Rejoice!" Help me find my joy in You alone, regardless of the trials I face, and let this joy be a testament to Your presence in my life.

Bless me with peace that surpasses understanding, as written in Philippians 4:7: "And the peace of God, which transcends all understanding, will guard your hearts and your minds in Christ Jesus." May Your peace dwell richly in my heart and mind, providing calm and assurance amidst life's uncertainties.

Instil in me forbearance—patience and endurance in times of testing. Help me to remain steadfast and compassionate towards others, as Your Word teaches in James 1:3-4: "Because you know that the testing of your faith produces perseverance. Let perseverance finish its work so that you may be mature and complete, not lacking anything." May I embrace challenges with a spirit of patience and grace.

Develop in me kindness and goodness that reflect Your character. Let my actions be a reflection of Your grace and moral excellence, as instructed in Ephesians 4:32: "Be kind and compassionate to one another, forgiving each other, just as in Christ God forgave you." May my kindness be evident in all my dealings, and my goodness inspire others to seek You.

Strengthen my faithfulness, Lord, that I may remain true to Your promises and faithful in my commitments. As Your Word says in 1 Corinthians 4:2: "Now it is required that those who have been given a trust must prove faithful." Help me to be reliable and steadfast, embodying Your faithfulness in all that I do.

Grant me gentleness, allowing me to approach others with humility and tenderness. Teach me to respond to challenges with a gentle spirit, as Galatians 6:1 instructs: "Brothers and sisters, if someone is caught in a sin, you who live by the Spirit should restore that person gently. But watch yourselves, or you also may be tempted." May my gentleness be a source of healing and encouragement.

Finally, empower me with self-control to manage my desires and actions in accordance with Your will. Help me to resist temptation and live a disciplined life that honours You, as stated in Proverbs 25:28: "Like a city whose walls are broken through is a person who lacks self-control." Grant me the strength to exercise self-control and live a life that is pleasing to You.

Father, I claim these qualities as written in Your Word, trusting that as I bear the Fruit of the Spirit, I will reflect Your love, grace, and power to the world around me. May Your Spirit work within me to manifest these virtues, bringing glory to Your name and drawing others closer to You.

In the mighty name of Jesus,
Amen.

Verse

Galatians 5:22-23 (NIV):

> *"But the fruit of the Spirit is love, joy, peace, forbearance, kindness, goodness, faithfulness, gentleness and self-control. Against such things there is no law."*

✹✹✹

Let the fruit of the Spirit guide your steps, for in love, joy, peace, and grace, you will find the true reflection of God's heart.

Daily Reflection

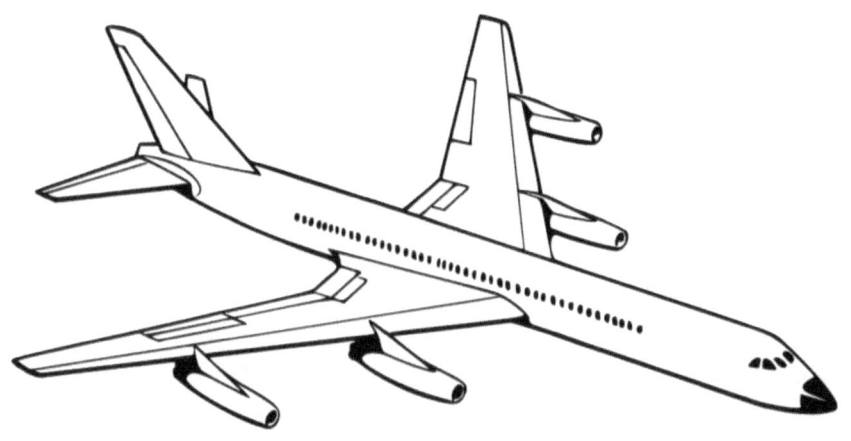

Prayer for my Strength and Support as a Fly In-Fly Out Worker (FIFO)

Word of Encouragement

Dear Friend,

As you read these words of prayer, know that you are surrounded by a wave of support and divine grace. The path you walk as a fly-in, fly-out worker comes with its unique set of challenges, but remember that God's presence is with you every step of the way. Your dedication and sacrifices are seen and valued, not only by those around you but by the One who sustains and strengthens you.

In the midst of weariness and long hours, hold firm to the truth that God's wisdom and peace are available to you at all times. Lean into His promises, and trust that He will guide you through each decision and challenge with clarity and strength. Your patience and perseverance are not in vain; they are building character and resilience that will bear fruit in time.

Take comfort in knowing that your family is supported by God's loving care as well. Their understanding and support reflect the strength of your bond, even in the face of physical separation. Cherish the moments you share and know that your sacrifices are meaningful and appreciated. God is working in both your life and theirs, weaving together moments of connection and joy.

As you navigate the complexities of your role, remember that you are not alone. God's protection surrounds you; His grace upholds you, and His love guides you. Keep your focus on Him, and let His strength be made perfect in your weakness. Trust in His timing and His plans, knowing that He is working all things together for your good.

May you find renewal and encouragement in the knowledge that God's love endures forever, and His promises are sure. Keep pressing forward with hope and confidence, for He is with you, guiding you, and blessing you in every season.

With heartfelt encouragement and prayers for your journey.

Prayer for my Strength and Support as a Fly In-Fly Out Worker (FIFO)

Our Dear Heavenly Father,

I come before You today with a heart full of gratitude and a deep need for Your strength and guidance. As I navigate the demands of my fly-in, fly-out work, I seek Your protection, wisdom, and peace. Lord, You are my refuge and strength, an ever-present help in times of trouble (Psalm 46:1). I trust in Your ability to sustain me through the weariness and exhaustion I face.

Father, grant me wisdom and discernment in every decision I make, ensuring that I act with integrity and clarity. Your Word says, "If any of you lacks wisdom, you should ask God, who gives generously to all without finding fault, and it will be given to you" (James 1:5). I ask for Your guidance in managing the complexities of my work and balancing my responsibilities.

Lord, fill my heart with inner peace amidst the challenges of my job. Your invitation to the weary comforts me: "Come to Me, all you who are weary and burdened, and I will give you rest" (Matthew 11:28). May Your peace guard my heart and mind, even in the midst of long hours and demanding tasks.

Grant me patience and perseverance to endure the trials and stresses of my work. Let me be steadfast in my efforts, knowing that "weeping may endure for a night, but joy comes in the morning" (Psalm 30:5). Strengthen my resolve to remain focused and concentrated, completing my tasks with diligence and excellence.

Help me to maintain a healthy work-life balance, managing my time effectively to ensure that I remain present for my loved ones and take care of my well-being. Your Word reminds us,

"There is a time for everything, and a season for every activity under the heavens" (Ecclesiastes 3:1). Guide me in finding the right balance and managing my time wisely.

Grant me emotional resilience to handle the pressures and challenges that come my way. Let Your strength be made perfect in my weakness, as Your Word says, "But He said to me, 'My grace is sufficient for you, for My power is made perfect in weakness'" (2 Corinthians 12:9). Let Your grace uphold me and give me the courage to face each day with renewed hope.

I also lift up my family to You, Father. I ask for Your blessings upon them as they navigate the challenges of our time apart. Grant them understanding, patience, and love, knowing that they, too, bear the weight of this separation. Help them to feel Your presence and comfort and let them experience the peace that surpasses all understanding (Philippians 4:7). May they find solace in Your promises and strength in Your grace.

Lord, help my family to remain united and supportive, even when we are apart. Strengthen our bond and deepen our love for one another, despite the physical distance. May our home be filled with understanding and compassion, as we all bear the weight of this separation. Provide them with the emotional support and encouragement they need and let them feel appreciated and valued.

Help them to manage their own challenges and find joy in the moments we do share. Let them know how much I cherish them and how deeply I long to be present in their lives. May our time together be filled with meaningful connections and moments of joy, strengthening our family ties despite the distance.

I pray for their well-being, that they may experience Your grace and favour in their own lives. May they see the purpose and value in the sacrifices we make and continue to support one another with unwavering love and commitment. Surround them with Your protection and keep them safe from harm.

I pray for recognition and appreciation in my work, not only from others but also from myself. Help me to find value and purpose in what I do, and may I remember that "whatever you do, work at it with all your heart, as working for the Lord" (Colossians 3:23). Let Your favour shine upon my efforts and let me see the fruits of my labour.

Most importantly, Lord, protect me and keep me safe as I work away from home. Surround me with Your angels and guard me from harm. Your Word promises, "He will command His angels concerning you to guard you in all your ways" (Psalm 91:11). I trust in Your protection and ask for Your continued watchful care.

Thank You, Father, for Your unwavering support and guidance. I place my trust in Your promise that You are working all things for my good (Romans 8:28). Bless me and my family with Your grace, peace, and strength as we navigate this journey together.

In Jesus' precious name, I pray,
Amen.

Verse

Numbers 6:24-26:

> *"The Lord bless you and keep you; the Lord make His face shine upon you and be gracious to you; the Lord turn His face toward you and give you peace."*

✯ ✯ ✯

May God's grace sustain us through every journey, keeping our hearts connected and our spirits strong, even in the midst of separation.

Daily Reflection

The Importance of Praise, Worship, and Prayer

As you journey through the pages of *Let's Pray About It,* you will discover the transformative power of prayer in every aspect of life. Prayer is our direct line of communication with God, a lifeline that provides comfort, guidance, and strength. It allows us to pour out our hearts, express our deepest desires, and seek divine intervention.

However, prayer is only one part of a vibrant spiritual life. Praise and worship are equally essential, as they draw us closer to God and foster a deeper connection with Him. Praise is our way of expressing gratitude for God's goodness and acknowledging His mighty works. Worship, on the other hand, is a profound act of reverence and adoration, an opportunity to honour God for who He is.

Why We Should Praise and Worship

Acknowledging God's Greatness

Praise and worship remind us of God's omnipotence, His incredible love, and His faithfulness. When we praise, we shift our focus from our problems to God's greatness, finding reassurance in His unchanging nature. As Psalm 150:6 says, "Let everything that has breath praise the Lord. Praise the Lord!"

Deepening Our Relationship with God

Worship fosters intimacy with God. When we come before Him with a heart full of adoration, we draw closer to His presence, experiencing His peace and joy. Jesus emphasised worshipping in spirit and truth in John 4:24: "God is spirit, and his worshipers must worship in the Spirit and in truth."

Strengthening Our Faith

Through praise and worship, we reaffirm our trust in God's promises. Singing songs of praise and meditating on His attributes reinforce our faith, especially during challenging times. Psalm 22:3 tells us that God inhabits the praises of His people, assuring us of His constant presence.

Renewing Our Minds

Worship has the power to transform our thoughts and attitudes. When we focus on God's goodness and mercy, our minds are renewed, and we find hope and encouragement. Romans 12:2 encourages us: "Do not conform to the pattern of this world but be transformed by the renewing of your mind."

Embracing a Life of Praise, Worship, and Prayer

Incorporating praise, worship, and prayer into our daily lives creates a balanced and fulfilling spiritual practice. It helps us maintain a positive outlook, strengthens our faith, and keeps us anchored in God's truth. As you read through *Let's Pray About It*, remember to lift your voice in praise and worship, complementing your prayers with heartfelt adoration and gratitude. This holistic approach will enrich your spiritual journey, providing you with the resilience and peace needed to navigate life's challenges.

May your time with this book deepen your relationship with God, bringing you comfort, strength, and unwavering hope.

A Special Message to You

Word of Encouragement

Dear Friend,

As you journey through these pages, know that you are not alone. Each word and prayer is a testament to the unwavering love and grace of our Heavenly Father. No matter what challenges you face, remember that God's presence is always with you, offering solace, strength, and hope.

In moments of struggle, let these prayers be your shield, and in times of darkness, let them be your guiding light. Trust in God's promises, for He is faithful and just. Lean on His strength and allow His peace to fill your heart, knowing that He is always there to lift you up and carry you through.

May your heart overflow with songs of praise, and may your worship draw you ever closer to the One who loves you beyond measure. Embrace the healing and wholeness that comes from walking in faith, and let your spirit be renewed by the profound love and joy that God offers.

Remember, incorporate the use of anointing oil, fasting, and prayer into your spiritual practices. These practices deepen your connection with God, bringing you closer to His guidance and experiencing His transformative presence in your life.

You are cherished, you are valued, and you are loved by an everlasting God. Keep your faith strong, and may your journey be filled with His abundant blessings.

With love and prayers,

Pamela Govender

My Prayer for You

Our Dear Heavenly Father,

As those who turn these pages seeking solace and strength, I ask for Your comforting presence to envelop them. May these prayers become their refuge in times of struggle and their beacon in moments of darkness. Grant them healing from their daily battles, whether physical, emotional, or spiritual. Renew their hope, fortify their resolve, and fill their hearts with Your enduring peace. In Your mercy, bring them restoration and wholeness as they walk this journey of faith.

Fill their hearts with songs of praise, lifting their voices to glorify Your name and acknowledge Your greatness. Let their worship draw them closer to You, deepening their relationship and allowing them to experience Your profound love and joy. May their praise and worship be a testament to Your faithfulness, transforming their spirits and renewing their minds.

In Jesus' precious name, I pray,

Amen.

Verse

Isaiah 43:2

> "When you pass through the waters, I will be with you; and through the rivers, they shall not overwhelm you; when you walk through fire you shall not be burned, and the flame shall not consume you."

Matthew 28:20

> "I am with you always, even to the end of the age."

Psalm 23:4

> "Even though I walk through the darkest valley, I will fear no evil, for you are with me; your rod and your staff, they comfort me."

***

Through every trial and triumph, remember: God's love surrounds you; His strength upholds you, and His presence never leaves you.

Let's Pray About It: A Powerful Way to Overcome Life's Struggles

As we conclude this journey together, I want to leave you with this enduring truth: prayer is our greatest tool in navigating life's challenges. Through prayer, we find solace, strength, and guidance. It connects us intimately with our Heavenly Father, who promises to be with us through every trial and triumph.

Remember, when we turn to Jesus in prayer, we tap into His endless grace and wisdom. He is our constant companion, ready to lift us up, comfort us, and lead us through every valley. As you face the days ahead, may you find peace in knowing that God is always near, ready to walk with you through whatever comes your way.

May your heart be filled with faith, your spirit renewed with hope, and your life enriched by the power of prayer and worship. Embrace the practice of anointing oil, fasting, and prayer as ways to draw closer to God. Claim and stand on God's Word as you pray, allowing His promises to guide and strengthen you. Through this, you will not only experience His transformative presence but also grow in your knowledge and understanding of His Word.

With heartfelt blessings.

Daily Reflection

Daily Reflection

Daily Reflection

Daily Reflection

Daily Reflection

Daily Reflection

Daily Reflection

Daily Reflection

Daily Reflection

Daily Reflection

Daily Reflection

Daily Reflection

Daily Reflection

Daily Reflection

Daily Reflection

About the Author

Pamela Govender is a dedicated author with a heart committed to helping others find their way through faith. Her career has been marked by guiding individuals in both their personal and professional development, always with a focus on compassionate support.

Pamela previously authored the insightful book *I Smiled Today*, which addresses themes of grieving and mourning. This work showcases her ability to provide comfort and understanding, offering readers a path to healing during times of loss.

In this latest book, *Let's Pray About It*, Pamela offers a heartfelt prayer guide designed to support readers through every situation they encounter in life. Each prayer is thoughtfully accompanied by a word of encouragement, providing readers with both spiritual comfort and practical guidance. As you pray, you will claim and stand on God's Word, deepening your understanding of the Bible with each prayer. Inspired by her own spiritual journey and the challenges she has faced, Pamela's prayers offer solace, hope, and a deeper connection with God. Her deep understanding of the transformative power of faith shines through on every page, making her work a beacon of light for those seeking strength and peace.

Through *Let's Pray About It,* Pamela Govender extends her compassionate touch, helping readers find solace, strength, and a more profound relationship with God by standing on His promises and learning His Word as they pray.

www.ingramcontent.com/pod-product-compliance
Lightning Source LLC
Chambersburg PA
CBHW030303080526
44584CB00012B/427